The Bedford Glossary
for World History

The Bedford Glossary for World History

Bedford/St. Martin's

Boston ◆ New York

For Bedford/St. Martin's

Publisher for History: Mary V. Dougherty
Executive Editor for History: Traci Mueller
Director of Development for History: Jane Knetzger
Senior Editor: Heidi L. Hood
Developmental Editor: Shannon Hunt
Editorial Assistant: Jennifer Jovin
Production Editor: Lidia MacDonald-Carr
Production Supervisor: Samuel Jones
Executive Marketing Manager: Jenna Bookin Barry
Cover Design: Richard DiTomassi
Text Design: Gretchen Toles
Composition: Eisner/Martin Typographics
Printing and Binding: Malloy Lithographing, Inc.

President: Joan E. Feinberg
Editorial Director: Denise B. Wydra
Director of Marketing: Karen R. Soeltz
Director of Editing, Design, and Production: Marcia Cohen
Assistant Director of Editing, Design, and Production: Elise S. Kaiser
Managing Editor: Elizabeth M. Schaaf

Library of Congress Control Number: 2009924656

Manufactured in the United States of America.

4 3 2 1 0 9
f e d c b a

For information, write: Bedford/St. Martin's, 75 Arlington Street, Boston, MA 02116   (617-399-4000)

ISBN-10: 0–312–57641–2
ISBN-13: 978–0–312–57641–7

Preface

The Bedford Glossary for World History offers students clear, concise definitions of terms they need to know in order to get the most from a world history course. This portable volume contains vocabulary that students will encounter in their reading for the survey as well as in contemporary media, enabling them to participate knowledgeably in discussions inside and outside the classroom. The terms are arranged alphabetically and cover political, economic, social, and cultural topics. Definitions provide time periods and historical context to help students locate the terms in world history and comprehend their significance. Incorporating and expanding on the glossaries found in Bedford/St. Martin's world history survey texts—*A History of World Societies* by John P. McKay, Bennett D. Hill, John Buckler, Patricia Buckley Ebrey, Roger B. Beck, Clare Haru Crowston, and Merry E. Wiesner-Hanks and *Ways of the World: A Brief Global History* by Robert W. Strayer—*The Bedford Glossary for World History* serves as a handy supplement for all versions of these books.

The Bedford Glossary
for World History

A

abolitionism An international movement that between approximately 1780 and 1890 succeeded in abolishing slavery in much of the world. Abolitionism drew inspiration from both the religious principles of Christianity and the secular thinking of the Enlightenment, an intellectual movement that began in Western Europe in the late seventeenth century and stressed the power of human reason and tolerance as well as the inherent nature of human rights.

absolutism A system of government in which a monarch holds sole and uncontestable power over the state and his or her subjects. European monarchs in the sixteenth and seventeenth centuries based their authority on the doctrine of the divine right of kings, which held that monarchs received their authority from God and were responsible only to Him.

acquired immunodeficiency syndrome (AIDS) A sexually transmitted disease, first reported in 1981, affecting tens of millions of people globally and the fourth-leading cause of death in the world. Caused by the human immunodeficiency virus (HIV), the epidemic has been concentrated in sub-Saharan Africa, but it has acquired a global presence with major outbreaks in Russia, South Asia, Southeast Asia, and elsewhere. Other diseases, extreme poverty, and political instability that results in the breakdown of basic health-care services and kinship networks have all contributed to the spread of AIDS in Africa and other impoverished regions of the world.

African diaspora *See* diaspora.

African National Congress (ANC) A South African political party established in 1912 by elite Africans who sought to win full acceptance in colonial society. It gradually became a popular movement and adopted more aggressive strategies in the struggle against apartheid. In South Africa's first multiracial elections in 1994, the ANC came to power under the leadership of President Nelson Mandela (r. 1994–1999). *See also* apartheid.

Afrikaners Also known as Boers, the descendants of Dutch colonists in what is now South Africa. The term "Afrikaner" suggests that they saw themselves as "white Africans," not just settlers but permanent inhabitants, and differentiated themselves from white South Africans of British descent, with whom Afrikaners clashed. From 1910 to 1994, this white minority dominated South African government and denied political rights to the black majority under the system of apartheid. *See also* apartheid.

Age of Revolution   *See* Atlantic revolutions.

age-grade   *See* age-set system.

age-set system   Among Bantu-speaking peoples and the Masai of East Africa, a system that initiated a group of young men from different villages and families into adulthood at the same time. This age set then rose together through a series of age grades, ranks or positions from junior warrior to senior elder. In some places women had their own corresponding age set and age grades. This system encouraged community-wide loyalties and cooperation.

agora   The central market square of the Greek city-state and an important feature of social and commercial life in ancient Greece, where people shopped or gathered for conversation. Public buildings within the agora, designed to facilitate this communal assembly, were built by wealthy elites who wished to demonstrate their own status.

Agricultural Revolution   An epic transformation of human life from a gathering and hunting economy to one that involved the deliberate cultivation of particular plants and the taming and breeding of particular animals. Also known as the Neolithic Revolution, this transformation occurred separately and independently in various locations in the Middle East, Asia, Africa, and the Americas between about 10,000 B.C.E. and 3000 B.C.E.

AIDS   *See* acquired immunodeficiency syndrome.

alphabetic script   A type of writing with a limited number of characters, each one representing a single sound. This innovation by the Phoenicians was adapted by the Greeks for their own language and subsequently by the missionary Cyril for the Slavic language.

al-Qaeda   An international organization of fundamentalist Islamic militants, formed around 1990 and headed by Osama bin Laden. It claimed responsibility for the attacks of September 11, 2001, on New York City and Washington, D.C., as well as other terrorist acts.

alternate globalization   *See* antiglobalization.

amir *See* emir.

Anabaptism A religious sect started in sixteenth-century Zurich, Switzerland, that believed that true faith was based on reason and free will and that people must not be baptized as infants, but instead knowingly select the Christian faith through baptism as adults. Anabaptists rebaptized adult followers and refused to have their children baptized; they also rejected the authority of the state and the courts, abolished private property, and believed themselves to be true Christians who lived according to the standards of the Bible. Considered heretics by other mainstream Christians of the time, Anabaptists were persecuted by both Catholic and Protestant authorities.

anarchism The belief that government is unnecessary and oppressive and should be replaced with voluntary cooperation and free association of people. As a political movement, it emerged in the nineteenth century and was popular among some peasants and workers who felt oppressed by their governments and large landowners. Anarchism was embraced by early labor unions, especially after they were outlawed in Russia and across Europe after 1850.

ANC *See* African National Congress.

anticlericalism Opposition to religious authority, especially in public life. It featured prominently in the Protestant Reformation and in the political controversies and revolutions of many, primarily Catholic, countries. *See also* Protestant Reformation.

antiglobalization/alternate globalization A major international movement that opposes the development of a corporate-based global economy on the grounds that it makes the rich richer and keeps poor regions in poverty, while exploiting their labor and environments. Members of this movement staged massive protests at a 1999 meeting of the World Trade Organization in Seattle, Washington.

anti-Semitism Prejudice against Jews. Its history dates back to ancient times, when pagan cultures imposed economic, personal, and political restrictions on Jews because of their different faith. In the European Middle Ages (ca. 600–1400) Christians periodically launched violent pogroms against Jews. While the eighteenth-century Enlightenment helped Jews gain civil rights in some countries, hard economic times fueled anti-Jewish bias against those who had achieved success. By the nineteenth and twentieth centuries, anti-Semitism became a significant component of right-wing political and social movements, sometimes casting Jewish people as a separate race rather than as members of a religion and presenting them as a biological threat to society. *See also* Holocaust, New Christians, pogrom.

apartheid Afrikaans term meaning "separateness"; a system supported by the Afrikaner government of South Africa that strictly limited the social and political integration of whites and blacks, with the intention of creating a society dominated by whites. Though segregation was widespread prior to the middle of the twentieth century, it was not until the National Party came to power in 1948 that it was formally named and adopted. Apartheid laws were repealed in 1991. *See also* African National Congress, Afrikaners.

appeasement The strategy of preventing a war by making concessions for legitimate grievances. Although leaders believed in its promise to secure "peace in our time," Britain and France's use of appeasement in dealing with Nazi Germany in the 1930s proved unsuccessful.

Arianism A theological belief, originating with Arius (ca. 260–336 C.E.), a priest of Alexandria, which maintained that God created Jesus from nothing and then bestowed him with special status. Therefore, Jesus was not divine or identical in nature with his Father and had not coexisted with him eternally. Arianism was both popular and controversial in early Christian communities, prompting emperors to intervene in church affairs and condemn Arianism as heresy.

aristocracy A type of government in which only the elite members of society, designated as such by birth or wealth, exercise authority. The term can also refer to an elite social group with land-based wealth and often with a title of nobility.

arquebus An early firearm loaded through the muzzle and used from the fifteenth to the seventeenth centuries in China and Europe. Heavy, but portable, it was the predecessor to the musket and the rifle.

Arthashastra An Indian treatise on political, economic, and military matters, probably written in the second century. It outlined the proper training and conduct of a ruler and the relationship between ruler and subject.

ASEAN *See* Association of Southeast Asian Nations.

assimilation The process by which one group incorporates the cultural traditions of another group. For example, early Christian missionaries aimed to ease the conversion of pagan peoples by stressing similarities between the pagans' customs and beliefs and those of Christianity.

Association of Southeast Asian Nations (ASEAN) An organization formed in 1967 by the non-Communist nations in Southeast Asia (Indonesia, Malaysia, the Philippines, Singapore, and Thailand) to promote cooperation among themselves and to strive for peace and prosperity. It later expanded its membership and became a major trading network.

astrolabe An instrument, developed by Muslim navigators in the twelfth century, that allowed mariners to plot their latitude by determining the altitude of the sun and other celestial bodies.

Athenian democracy A form of direct democracy, developed around 500 B.C.E., in which much of the free male population of Athens had the right to vote and officeholders were chosen by lot.

Atlantic revolutions The period between 1770 and 1850 marked by a number of revolutions and rebellions on both sides of the Atlantic Ocean by countries, colonies, and peoples seeking independence. Such movements included the American Revolution (1775–1783), the French Revolution (1789–1815), the Haitian Revolution (1791–1804), and the Latin American struggles for independence (1810–1825).

Atlantic system The pattern of trade beginning in the 1500s that bound together Western Europe, Africa, and the Americas. Europeans traded goods for slaves from Western Africa and sold them in the Americas, where their labor produced commodities such as coffee and sugar that were then sold at European ports for refinement or reshipment. The Atlantic system also provided new markets for items manufactured in Europe, often using raw materials produced on plantations in the Americas by slave labor.

atman In classic Hindu belief, the immortal human soul, or "true self" that seeks union with Brahman and is identical with Brahman. In traditional Buddhism, the existence of such a solid and coherent "self" is generally denied.

audiencia The twelve to fifteen judges who served as an advisory council and as the highest judicial body in a Spanish colony.

They were established in the sixteenth century and presided over by the viceroy, who served as the colonial representative for the Spanish monarchy. *See also* viceroyalty.

Ausgleich German for "compromise"; an agreement made in 1867 that joined the countries of Austria and Hungary. They each maintained a separate legislature and constitution but were united under a dual monarchy.

Australopithecus The earliest ancestor of humans that had characteristics distinct from those of apes. It lived in Africa from 1.5 to 4 million years ago.

Austronesian migrations The last phase of the great human migration that established a human presence in every habitable region of the earth. Austronesian-speaking people settled the Pacific islands and Madagascar in a series of seaborne migrations that began around 3,500 years ago, ensuring their survival by the mastery of agriculture.

authoritarianism A form of government in which a ruler tries to maintain the existing social order using obedient armies, police, and government officials to suppress dissent and attempts at liberal reform.

Avesta A collection of the ancient holy scriptures of Zoroastrianism, a religion that took root in Persia between 558 and 330 B.C.E. *See also* Zoroastrianism.

Axis The World War II (1939–1945) alliance created in 1936 between Italy, Germany, and Japan and their client states. Axis members pledged to support each other's aggressive military campaigns.

ayllu A self-sustaining kinship group that shared land and served as the fundamental social unit of society during the Inca Empire (1438–1533).

B

Babylonian Captivity A period of time between 587 and 537 B.C.E. when the survivors of an attack by Nebuchadnezzer on the southern kingdom of Judah were sent into exile in Babylonia. The term was later used to refer to the seventy years (1307–1377) when the popes of the Catholic Church resided in Avignon, France, instead of in Rome, Italy.

bakufu The military government established in Japan in the twelfth century, in which the emperor and his civil government remained, but real power was concentrated in a shogun, or general-in-chief.

balance of power A diplomatic arrangement in which states band together to maintain peace among themselves and form a greater force against a potential enemy.

Balfour Declaration A 1917 statement by British foreign secretary Arthur Balfour that supported the idea of a Jewish homeland in Palestine. The declaration was meant to appeal to Jews in Germany, Austria, and the United States; some British officials believed this would help their war effort, and others claimed that such a homeland, grateful to the British for its creation, would help Great Britain maintain control of the Suez Canal. Jews who did settle in Palestine, however, faced bitter resentment from Arabs in Palestine, and anti-Jewish riots ensued.

banner A unit of the Chinese Manchu army, reorganized under the Qing dynasty (1644–1911) in the late sixteenth century. Each was made up of a set of military companies but included the families and slaves of the soldiers as well.

baroque An artistic style with ties to the Catholic Reformation that emerged in Rome in the seventeenth century. It was meant to reaffirm the emotional depths of the Catholic faith and to glorify both the church and the monarchy. Baroque art is characterized by emotional intensity, exaggerated lighting, release from restraint, and even a kind of artistic sensationalism—a departure from the classical art of the Renaissance, which emphasized harmonious and precise design, unity, and clarity. *See also* classicism.

Battle of Talas River An Arab victory over the Chinese in 751 C.E. that checked Chinese expansion to the west and enabled the conversion of Central Asia to Islam.

bazaar economy A traditional economy with few salaried jobs and an abundance of tiny, unregulated businesses such as peddlers and pushcart operators. In modern times, bazaar economies became common in urban areas of developing countries as the gap between rich and poor widened.

benefice A system of church offices supported by an endowment. In essence, benefices are stipends paid to clergy in exchange for performing religious duties such as holding mass; particularly in medieval Europe, benefices were issued in the form of land grants. The holding of vast and multiple benefices in the Catholic Church led to abuse and secular and religious conflicts.

Berlin Conference An international conference held in 1884 and 1885 to lay down basic rules for imperialist competition in sub-Saharan Africa. It established the principle that European claims to African territory had to rest on "effective occupation" to be recognized by other states. As a result, several European countries launched aggressive campaigns to extend their current coastal holdings into the interior. The conference also agreed to prohibit the slave trade in Africa. *See also* scramble for Africa.

Berlin Wall A twenty-eight-mile concrete wall topped with barbed wire, built by the Soviet Union in 1961 along the border of East and West Berlin to prevent East Germans from leaving for the West. It became emblematic of the cold war and the division of Europe until its breaching in 1989 amid the overthrow of communist governments all across Eastern Europe.

bhakti An immensely popular religious movement in Hinduism, advocating intense devotion toward a particular deity through songs, prayer, and rituals. In India, Buddhism was almost entirely absorbed as another bhakti cult by 1000 C.E.

Black Consciousness movement A South African movement that sought to foster pride, unity, and political awareness among the country's African majority and often resorted to violent protest against white minority rule. Black Consciousness gained popularity in the 1960s in the midst of the government's violent reaction to peaceful protests by the African National Congress. *See also* African National Congress.

Black Death The name later given to the massive pandemic that swept through Eurasia and North Africa beginning in 1331 and reached a peak in 1347–1351, killing a third to a half of the population of Europe and shaking the foundations of medieval society. The Black Death is traditionally regarded as an outbreak of bubonic plague, carried by rats and their fleas from ship to port to city, although some recent historians have claimed the massive death toll was due to a combination of epidemic diseases. *See also* bubonic plague.

Black Shirts A private army formed under Italy's dictator Benito Mussolini (r. 1922–1945) in the 1920s that destroyed socialist newspapers, union halls, and Socialist Party headquarters, eventually pushing Socialists out of the city governments of northern Italy.

blitzkrieg German for "lightning war"; a new military strategy first used by Germany in World War II (1939–1945) that involved the rapid movement of infantry, tanks, and airpower over large areas. The overwhelmed enemy was left in a state of shock, unable to resist psychologically or militarily.

Bloody Sunday In Russia, a massacre of peaceful protesters at Winter's Square in Saint Petersburg in 1905. It turned ordinary workers against the tsar and produced a wave of general anger and discontent, setting the stage for the Russian Revolution of 1905. *See also* Russian Revolution of 1905.

bodhisattva In Mahayana Buddhism, an enlightened being who delays entry into nirvana and chooses to remain in the world of suffering to assist others in their quest for salvation.

Boer War The war between British and Boer (Dutch-descended) inhabitants of South Africa for control of the region, which lasted from 1899 to 1902. Although it played upon British imperialist fervor, the war's heavy casualties and bloodshed, as well as the unfit conditions of British soldiers and inhumane treatment of South Africans, subsequently convinced many British people that empire was morally wrong, or at least too costly to maintain.

Bolshevik A faction of the Social Democratic Party in Russia, led by Vladimir Lenin (r. 1917–1924), that seized power in 1917. Unlike most Marxists, who believed in the power of laboring people, Lenin stressed that a highly disciplined socialist elite—rather than the working class as a whole—would lead Russia to socialism. The term comes from the Russian word for "majority," though at that time, the Bolsheviks were often in the minority. The Bolsheviks later became the Communist Party in Russia. *See also* Marxism.

Book of the Dead An Egyptian book that preserved people's ideas about death and the afterlife. It explains that after death, the soul leaves the body to become part of the divine.

bourgeoisie The urban middle class, typically educated and prosperous. Karl Marx (1818–1883) also used the term to describe economic relationships under capitalism.

Boxer Rebellion An uprising of Chinese militia organizations in 1900 in which large numbers of Europeans and Chinese Christians were killed.

Boyars The highest-ranking members of the Russian nobility, just below royalty. Tsars depended on their military and political cooperation.

Brahma In Upanishadic Hindu belief, the final, unchanging reality or the "World Soul," a universal and eternal soul that binds all life forms together.

Brahmin The Indian social class of priests who supported the growth of royal power in return for royal confirmation of their own religious rights, power, and status. Brahmin was the highest varna in the caste system. *See also* caste system.

Bretton Woods system Named for a conference held at Bretton Woods, New Hampshire, in 1944, this system provided the foundation for postwar economic globalization, including the World Bank and the International Monetary Fund, and promoted free trade, stable currencies, and high levels of capital investment. *See also* World Bank.

Brezhnev Doctrine The doctrine created after the Soviet invasion of Czechoslovakia in 1968, according to which the Soviet Union and its allies had the right to intervene in any socialist country to protect and preserve a socialist system. Leonid Brezhnev (r. 1964–1982) and his conservative government feared that the "socialism with a human face" reforms undertaken by the Czech Communist Party, known as the "Prague Spring," challenged Communist rule itself. *See also* Prague Spring.

bride wealth A custom in some societies whereby at marriage, the groom paid the bride or her family a sum of money that remained under her control. This arrangement gave daughters a higher value than they had in patriarchal societies that required the bride's family to pay the groom a dowry.

British East India Company A private trading company chartered by Queen Elizabeth I of England (r. 1533–1603) around 1600, in response to the success of the Dutch East India Company. Initially its members were given a monopoly on Indian

Ocean trade, including the right to make war and to rule conquered peoples.

British Royal Society An association of scientists established in England in 1660 that was dedicated to the promotion of "useful knowledge." The society established technological libraries, held public lectures and demonstrations, and published broadsheets and pamphlets on scientific advances.

Bronze Age The period from around 4000 to 1000 B.C.E. that is considered the earliest era of civilization, in which the production and use of bronze implements became basic to society. Tools and weapons of bronze, an alloy of copper and tin, made farming more efficient and revolutionized warfare. In Europe and the Near East, the Bronze Age was marked by increasing divides between wealthy and poor and men and women. Bronze Age civilizations gradually became more complex, as long-distance commerce developed and rulers created legal systems to promote justice and solidify their own power.

bubonic plague A highly fatal disease transmitted by fleas that devastated the Mediterranean world between 534 and 750 C.E. and was most likely the disease referred to as the Black Death, which ravaged Europe, Asia, and Northern Africa between 1346 and 1350.

Buddhism A religion and cultural tradition founded in India by Siddhartha Gautama (the Buddha, or "enlightened one") around 500 B.C.E., which set forth the Four Noble Truths and a code of conduct, the Eightfold Path. Buddhism ignored India's strict caste system and held that anyone could achieve enlightenment by following the Eightfold Path. Buddhism entered China from India in the first and second centuries C.E., but only became popular in 300–800 C.E. through a series of cultural accommodations. The Mahayana form of Buddhism, a more popular form, spread to China, Korea, and Japan; the Theravada (traditional) form was practiced in India, Sri Lanka, and Southeast Asia; and the Tantric form in Tibet. *See also* Chan Buddhism, Eightfold Path, Four Noble Truths, Mahayana Buddhism, Theravada Buddhism.

burgher In medieval Europe, a male middle-class citizen residing in a town who enjoyed certain legal privileges, including the right to participate in town governance.

bushido Also called the "Way of the Warrior," a code of conduct by which Japanese samurai were expected to live. Bushido stressed the military values of bravery, loyalty, and death over surrender. *See also* samurai.

C

cabinet system A political system in which heads of governmental administrative departments serve as a group to advise the head of state. All these ministers are drawn from the majority party in the legislature and are responsible to it.

caesaropapism A political system in which the secular ruler is also head of the religious establishment, as during certain periods of the Byzantine Empire (330–1453). Caesaropapism was at the heart of the Investiture Conflict (1077–1122) between Pope Gregory VII (r. 1073–1085) and Holy Roman Emperor Henry IV (r. 1056–1105), who both believed they should have authority over the church; the result was that the Roman Catholic Church retained some degree of independence from political authorities in Europe. *See also* Investiture Conflict.

caliph A successor of the Prophet Muhammad (ca. 570–632 C.E.) following his death. Both religious and secular leaders, caliphs were originally selected from Muhammad's inner circle and were seen as the representatives or deputies of God. Disputes over the legitimacy of the succession of caliphs Uthman (644–656 C.E.) and Ali (656–661 C.E.) led to the schism between Sunni and Shia Muslims that continues today. *See also* Shia, Sunni.

calpulli A kinship group of the Aztec civilization (1345–1521) that also functioned as a political unit, paying taxes to the central government and providing the state with labor.

Calvinism A branch of Protestantism based on the ideas of John Calvin (1509–1564), who stressed the absolute power of God and the weakness of humans. Calvin believed in the doctrine of predestination, which states that human beings do not have free will and that God has already chosen who would be damned and who would be saved—meaning that men and women cannot achieve salvation through good deeds on Earth.

canon law The internal law of the Roman Catholic Church. Originally a loose collection of papal decrees and edicts from church councils about the rules and practice of the faith, canon law became a means through which the papacy asserted its authority over the church and medieval society.

capitalism An economic system in which the means of production—labor, machines, and financial investment—are controlled by private individuals or institutions for their own personal profit. Based on Adam Smith's 1776 work *The Wealth of Nations*, modern capitalism takes as its central tenet a belief in free enterprise—that is, that the market forces of supply and demand, and not government regulations, should be the determining factors in the economy. *See also* laissez-faire.

capitulations A series of agreements that basically surrender the rights of one party. In an effort to revive European trade, slowed by shifting trade routes, the Ottoman government signed capitulations with France, England, and the Habsburgs between 1536 and 1615, giving these Europeans a stranglehold on Ottoman trade and commerce.

caravan A group of merchants who transported their goods on the backs of camels and traveled together for protection against raiders. Camel caravans were used to cross the Sahara in North Africa and travel the Silk Roads in Central Asia. *See also* Silk Roads.

caravanserai Inns that catered to travelers on trade routes in North Africa, Asia, and southeastern Europe; they provided water and stalls for animals.

caravel A small, maneuverable, three-mast sailing ship developed by the Portuguese in the fifteenth century. The caravel gave the Portuguese a distinct advantage in exploration and trade.

Carolingian Renaissance The revival of learning inaugurated during the rule of Frankish king Charlemagne (r. 768–814) who controlled much of continental Europe. Its objective was to enhance the glory of the kings, educate their officials, reform the liturgy, and purify the Roman Catholic faith. Emphasis was placed on the preservation of Greek and Roman language, ideas, and achievements. The Carolingian Renaissance, which continued after Charlemagne's death, served as a model for the development of monastic schools and the revival of learning that occurred in the twelfth century.

carrack A sailing ship with three or four masts, developed by the Portuguese in the fifteenth century as a suitable ocean-going ship. The Portuguese and the Spanish used carracks in their early exploration of the Atlantic world.

cartel A commercial association whose independent members join forces to fix prices or limit competition.

cash-crop agriculture Agricultural production, often on a large scale, of crops for sale in the market, rather than for consumption by the farmers themselves. Europeans encouraged cash-crop agriculture in their Asian and African colonies during the nineteenth and twentieth centuries.

caste system An Indian system that divided society into four hierarchical strata, called varna, that determined a person's position and status for life. People were born into the varna of Brahmin (priests), Kshatriya (warriors and rulers), Vaisya (farmers), or Sudra (subordinate native peoples). By medieval times, each of these groups was divided into occupation-based castes, called jatis, which had their own governing bodies.

Caste War of Yucatán The long revolutionary struggle (1847–1901) of the Maya people of Mexico against European and mestizo intruders.

Catholic Reformation *See* Counter-Reformation.

Catholicism A Western European branch of Christianity that gradually defined itself as separate from Eastern Orthodoxy, with a major break in 1054 C.E. in which the two branches excommunicated each other. "Roman Catholic" was not commonly used until after the Protestant Reformation, but by the eleventh century, Western Christendom defined itself in centralized terms, with the bishop of Rome (the pope) as the ultimate authority in matters of doctrine. Cardinals, who act as papal advisers, form the next level of the hierarchy, followed by bishops who are responsible for dioceses, and priests who are responsible for parishes within dioceses. *See also* Eastern Orthodoxy, Great Schism.

caudillo A military strongman who seized control of a government in nineteenth-century Latin America. Within the extremely unstable political atmosphere, leadership changed hands frequently.

censor In ancient Rome, a government official who held a number of responsibilities that included supervising morals, determining who could lawfully sit in the senate, registering citizens, and leasing public contracts.

censorate One of the ministries of the Chinese government, responsible for checking the effectiveness of officials and reporting misconduct to the emperor. The branch originated during the Qin dynasty (221–206 B.C.E.).

Chan Buddhism A school of Buddhism, originating in China in the eighth century, that emphasized salvation through personal conduct and discipline, meditation, and mystical enlightenment rather than scriptural knowledge and ritual performance. It was adopted by the Japanese in the twelfth century as Zen Buddhism.

chattel slavery The absolute legal ownership of another person, including the right to buy or sell that person.

Cheka The tsarist secret police, reestablished in 1917 after the Bolsheviks took power, which hunted down and executed thousands of real or suspected foes of communism, creating an environment of fear and silencing opposition.

chiefdom A form of political organization in which a hereditary leader, or chief, holds both political and religious authority and has special rights to the wealth of the community. The rank of its members is determined by their degree of kinship to the chief, and the chief typically relies on generosity, ritual status, or charisma rather than force to win obedience from the people.

chinampa An artificial terrace for farming and house-building constructed in the shallows of Mexico's Lake Texcoco. The people of the Aztec Empire (1345–1521) and their neighbors placed soil from the bottom of the lake onto mats of woven twigs and used the surface for growing crops.

Chinese Revolution The long revolutionary process during the period 1912–1949 that began with the overthrow of the Chinese imperial system and ended with the triumph of the Communist Party under the leadership of Mao Zedong (r. 1949–1976).

chivalry An ideal code of conduct toward which a medieval knight was supposed to strive, stressing the virtues of bravery, generosity, honor, graciousness, mercy, and gallantry toward women. Devised by the clergy in an attempt to refine the crude and brutal behavior of knights, the chivalric code encouraged skills such as conversation and dancing in addition to military might.

Christian humanists Scholars from northern Europe who, in the late fifteenth and early sixteenth centuries, developed programs for broad social reform based on concepts set forth in the Renaissance and on the ideals of the Christian faith, such as peace, morality, and virtue. They sought to realize the ethical ideals of the classical world and of the Bible.

city-state A state consisting of an urban center that exercises political and economic control over the countryside around it. Mesopotamian city-states, which first appeared around 3000 B.C.E., were marked by their strong fortification walls and large temples. The governments of these early city-states effectively organized and managed the labor used to maintain the increasingly complex irrigation systems around the Tigris and Euphrates rivers.

civil disobedience A political strategy of deliberately but peacefully breaking the law to protest oppression and obtain political change. Mohandas Gandhi (1869–1948) advocated civil disobedience in India's movement for independence from Britain.

civil service examinations A highly competitive series of tests, based on the Confucian classics, that were taken by those who wished to become officials in the Chinese government. The examinations provided a modest opportunity for advancement in society, as in theory any man could take them regardless of class. In practice, they were largely limited to those who could afford the expensive education that prepared candidates for these exams.

civilization A form of human society that featured powerful states, substantial urban centers, dense populations, large public buildings, diverse economies, sharply stratified societies, patriarchy, and some knowledge of writing. The very first civilizations—in Mesopotamia, Egypt, and Peru—emerged around 3500 B.C.E. to 3000 B.C.E.

classical liberalism A political system that emphasizes the protection of individual liberties and private property with safeguards against unchecked political power.

classicism An artistic style that reflected the ideals of the art of Greco-Roman antiquity and placed a high value on formality and order. Classicism during the European Renaissance in the fifteenth and sixteenth centuries and the eighteenth-century Enlightenment respectively prompted and reacted to the sensuous, exuberant, and emotional forms of the baroque. *See also* baroque.

client A free man or woman who was dependent on superiors (patrons) for his or her livelihood. In return for their labor and loyalty, clients might receive land, protection, gifts, or other favors from their patrons. *See also* patronage.

cold war A conflict conducted without direct military action; specifically, the rivalry between the Soviet Union and the United States that shaped world politics between 1945 and 1989. With both countries vying for dominance, the cold war divided the West, led to the massive growth of nuclear weapons, and caused acute anxiety in political circles and among the general population. It was a significant force in defining global political and economic relationships through the 1980s.

collective security The system of group diplomacy, especially involving the peaceful resolution of disputes, established by the League of Nations in January 1919 following World War I (1914–1918).

collectivization The process of rural reform undertaken by the Communist leadership of both the Soviet Union (beginning in 1929) and China (in the mid-1950s) in which private property rights in land were largely abolished. Peasants had to give up their individual plots of land as well as their tools and animals and join "collective farms," where they had to work cooperatively and share the proceeds as a community rather than as individuals. Collectivization in China occurred more easily and more rapidly than in the Soviet Union, where resistance was strong and peasants destroyed their livestock and crops rather than relinquish them to collective farms.

colonization The settlement of people from one country or region in another country or region. The term is sometimes used to indicate any kind of foreign control, as in the colonization of Africa during the nineteenth century.

Columbian exchange The massive transatlantic interaction and exchange of people, animals, plants, diseases, and ideas among the Americas, Africa, and Eurasia that took place during the several centuries following Christopher Columbus's historic voyage in 1492.

Comintern Short for "Communist International"; an association of Communist parties from various countries founded by Russian Bolshevik leader Vladimir Lenin (r. 1917–1924) in 1919 to promote the spread of revolution and the dissemination of Communist principles. Lenin insisted that all parties submit to its twenty-one points of doctrine, including dominance by Moscow, which ultimately caused controversy within the organization. *See also* Bolshevik.

Commercial Revolution The transformation of the economic structure of Europe, beginning in the eleventh century, from a rural, manorial society to a more complex mercantile society. The development of a profit-based economy, the growth of cities, increased trade, and the rise of powerful groups of merchants and artisans prompted the renewal of long-distance trade networks, new business arrangements, and greater agricultural production. The Commercial Revolution prompted the creation of important institutions such as corporations, banks, and accounting systems.

Common Market *See* European Economic Community (EEC).

commune A sworn association of citizens who formed a corporate legal body to govern their town independent of any monarch or lord. Especially prominent in eleventh-century Italy, communes became the normal institution of constitutional government in medieval towns, complete with their own courts of law. The term also refers to a group of people who share resources, as in the Jewish kibbutz or the communes of China's Great Leap Forward. *See also* Great Leap Forward, kibbutz.

communism A Marxist term referring to the final stage of human development (following that of socialism) in which social equality and collective living will be most fully developed. The term is also used to distinguish those political parties committed to revolution from those that believed that socialism could evolve peacefully within a democratic framework. *See also* socialism.

compass A tool developed sometime during the Song dynasty (960–1279) in China to aid in navigation at sea, consisting of a magnetic needle contained in a small protective case that pointed north. Arab traders brought the compass to Europe around the twelfth century.

Concert of Europe An agreement by the Great Powers of Europe—Great Britain, Prussia, Russia, Austria (and, after 1818, France)—following the Congress of Vienna in 1815 in which they agreed to act together on matters affecting all of them individually. The arrangement, which sought to maintain peace, the monarchy, and religious values, called for regular, informal meetings to maintain stability and special sessions in times of crisis to prevent European war. It helped maintain general peace during the revolutions of 1848. *See also* Congress of Vienna.

concubine A woman contracted to a man as one of multiple wives, who often lived in a harem with the man's mother, wife, unmarried sisters, and children. In the Ottoman Empire as well as in China, the sons of royal concubines had the potential to inherit their father's throne.

Confucianism A body of thought based on the ideas of the Chinese philosopher Confucius (551–479 B.C.E.) that advocated the moral example of superiors as the key element of social order. Imperial academies emphasized Confucian teachings, and admittance to the civil service required an extensive knowledge of his ideas.

Congress of Vienna A meeting among the powers allied against French emperor Napoleon I (r. 1804–1814)—Great Britain, Russia, Prussia, and Austria—that began shortly before his downfall in 1814 and lasted into the following year. Reactionary in many aspects, the Congress sought wherever possible to restore Europe to the way it was before the wars of the French Revolution (1789–1799) and Napoleon by returning many states to their traditional monarchs. The conservative Congress system, also called the "Congress of Europe," helped maintain peace in Europe until the 1850s. *See also* Concert of Europe, conservatism.

conquistadores Spanish for "conquerors"; sixteenth-century Spanish soldiers/explorers who sought to conquer the native peoples of the Americas and claim their land for the Spanish crown.

conservatism A political ideology favoring traditions such as religion and royalty and valuing the political rule of monarchs and the social dominance of an aristocracy.

Constantinople, fall of The surrender of Constantinople, the capital and almost the only outpost left of the Byzantine Empire (330–1453), in 1453 to the army of the Ottoman sultan Mehmed II "the Conqueror." The event marked the end of Christian Byzantium.

constitutional monarchy A form of government in which the king or queen retains his or her position as head of state, while the authority to tax and legislate new laws resides in an elected body. *See also* constitutionalism.

constitutionalism A form of government in which power is balanced between the authority and power of the government on the one hand, and the rights and liberties of the subject or citizen on the other hand. Rulers are required to share power with legislative bodies made up of elected representatives. Constitutionalism emerged in seventeenth-century Europe where it posed a great challenge to absolutism. *See also* absolutism.

consul A high-ranking executive authority in Rome, first established in the sixth century B.C.E. The title was revived during the French Revolution (1789–1799) in 1799; Napoleon Bonaparte (1769–1821) was known as First Consul.

Copernican hypothesis The theory that the earth and other planets revolve around a fixed sun, as set forth by the Polish astronomer Nicolaus Copernicus (1473–1543).

co-prosperity sphere A region of Asian states dominated by Japan during World War II (1939–1945) and which, in theory, benefited from Japan's superior civilization.

Coptic Christianity The Egyptian variety of Christianity, distinctive in its belief that Christ has only a single, divine nature.

corpus juris civilis Latin for the "body of civil law"; it is composed of three books—the *Code*, the *Digest*, and the *Institutes*, commissioned by the Roman/Byzantine emperor Justinian (r. 527–565)—and forms the basis of law in nearly every present-day European nation.

Counter-Reformation (Catholic Reformation) The sixteenth-century religious movement that arose within the Roman Catholic Church in response to the critiques of the Protestant Reformation. Like their Protestant counterparts, Catholic reformers sought to address corruption within the church; unlike Protestants, these reformers wanted to preserve Catholic theology and traditions. The church reasserted its doctrine at the Council of Trent, held intermittently from 1545–1563, during which reforms were established to end the sale of church offices and strengthen church structure.

coup d'état French for "stroke of state"; the overthrow of a government by violent means.

Covenant A formal agreement between Yahweh and the Hebrew people. In the ancient history of Israel and Judah, if the Hebrews worshipped Yahweh as their only god, he would consider them his chosen people, provide them with a homeland, and protect them from their enemies. *See also* Hebrews, Judaism.

Creoles Persons of Spanish or Portuguese descent born in the colonial Americas. Creoles resented the power of peninsulares, colonial officials born in Europe; wishing to be free from Spain and Portugal and supplant the peninsulares as the ruling class, they led a series of revolutions in Latin America between 1806 and 1825. *See also* peninsulares.

Crimean War A major international conflict (1854–1856) stemming from a dispute between France and Russia as to who should protect Christian holy places in the Ottoman Empire. Russia's subsequent attempt to annex parts of the Ottoman Empire prompted Great Britain and France to respond with force; aided by Sardinia and the Ottomans, they defeated Russia. Both sides suffered heavy casualties, but the loss prompted reforms within Russia, including the freeing of the serfs in 1861, and a British movement for nursing reform.

crossbow A weapon developed in China during the Warring States Period (500–221 B.C.E.) that allowed foot soldiers to shoot farther than horsemen carrying light bows. To defend themselves against crossbow bolts, soldiers began to wear armor and helmets.

Crusades A series of military campaigns instigated by the Roman papacy with the goal of returning Jerusalem and other holy places in Palestine to Christian rule. Eight major crusades were fought between 1096 and the end of the thirteenth century. The First Crusade succeeded in capturing Jerusalem in 1099, but Muslim armies reconquered all of the Christian territories by 1291.

Cuban missile crisis A major standoff between the United States and the Soviet Union in 1962 over Soviet installation of medium-range nuclear missiles in Cuba, just off the U.S. coast. After thirteen tense days in which nuclear war seemed possible, the confrontation ended in compromise, with the USSR removing its missiles in exchange for the United States agreeing not to invade Cuba. *See also* cold war.

cult The devotions and rituals surrounding a particular symbol or aspect of a larger religious tradition, or the group that performs those devotions and rituals.

Cultural Revolution A Chinese Communist program launched by Mao Zedong (r. 1949–1976) in the 1960s in order to combat the capitalist tendencies that he believed reached into even the highest ranks of the Communist Party. The program was carried out by young people with great violence; in their attempt to remake Chinese thought, behavior, and everyday life, they threw China into chaos.

Culture System   The Dutch policy instituted in 1830 that required Indonesian peasants to plant a fifth of their land in export crops, which were then turned over to the Dutch as taxes.

cuneiform   From the Latin for "wedge-shaped"; a form of writing that used wedge-shaped symbols for words and syllables. The Sumerians first developed cuneiform around 3500 B.C.E. to document their increasingly complex economic transactions.

curacas   The headman of a clan in the Inca Empire (1438–1533), who was responsible for conducting relations with outsiders.

Cyrillic script   An alphabet based on Greek letters that was developed by two Byzantine missionaries, Cyril (826–869) and Methodius (815–885), in order to write Slavic languages. Cyrillic script made possible the birth of Russian literature. *See also* alphabetic script.

D

daimyo Feudal lords of Japan who ruled with virtual independence thanks to their bands of samurai warriors. Beginning amidst political turmoil in the sixteenth century, the daimyo ruled without much interference by the government until the Meiji restoration of 1868. *See also* samurai.

Daodejing The central text of Daoism, translated as *The Way and Its Power*. *See also* Daoism.

Daoism A Chinese philosophy and popular religion that advocates simplicity and immersion in the world of nature. Daoists disagreed with followers of Confucius (551–479 B.C.E.), who sought to make the government work for the people, instead placing a high value on private life and opposing government interference. *See also* Confucianism.

Dawes Plan The product of a post–World War I (1914–1918) reparations commission, accepted by Germany, France, and Britain, that reduced Germany's yearly reparations, made the payments dependent on German economic prosperity, and granted Germany large loans from the United States to promote its recovery.

Declaration of the Rights of Man and Citizen A decree granting basic rights to French citizens that was written in August 1789, at the beginning of the French Revolution (1789–1799), as a preamble to France's constitution. Reminiscent of the American Declaration of Independence, this document established the sovereignty of the nation, meaning that the king derived his authority from the people of the nation rather than from divine right or tradition. Women were theoretically citizens under civil law but did not have the right to full political participation. Slaves were also overlooked in the Declaration.

decolonization The reversal of Europe's overseas expansion caused by the rising demand of colonized Asian, African, and Middle Eastern peoples for national self-determination, racial equality, and personal dignity. After World War II (1939–1945), most European powers were willing to let go of their colonies and focus on rebuilding their own countries, though they still wanted to maintain some ties with the colonies. While most countries gained their independence by negotiated settlement with gradual political reforms, some, such as Mozambique, Algeria, and Vietnam, had to engage in prolonged military conflict.

deforestation The cutting down of forests, usually to clear land for farming and human settlement. Deforestation was a necessary part of agricultural revolution; however, excessive deforestation in modern times has contributed to global warming.

deism The belief that a benevolent, all-knowing God designed the universe and set it in motion, but no longer intervenes in its functioning or in human affairs. Deism emerged in the West during the eighteenth-century Enlightenment, as scientists and philosophers discovered natural explanations for how the universe operated that did not rely on divine intervention.

Delian League The naval alliance of city-states headed by Athens after Greek victory in the Greco-Persian Wars (499–479 B.C.E.), prompted by the fear of further hostility and invasion. Named for the island of Delos where its treasury was kept, the Delian League came to be dominated by Athenians, who used its revenue to glorify their city.

demesne In feudal Europe, the land attached to a manor or estate and cultivated by peasants, or serfs, on the lord's behalf. *See also* manorialism.

democracy From the Greek for "the power of the people"; a type of government in which all citizens, without regard to birth or wealth, administer the workings of government. Democracy in ancient Athens opened political participation to all free men, but still excluded women, slaves, and foreigners.

de-Stalinization The liberalization of the Soviet Union following the death of Joseph Stalin (r. 1929–1953), led by reformer Nikita Khrushchev (r. 1953–1964). The process included diverting resources from heavy industry and the military to consumer goods and agriculture. Controls over workers relaxed; people were freed from the gulag, the network of prison camps; and the standard of living slowly improved.

détente From the French for "loosening" or "relaxing"; an easing of tensions between two rivals. Specifically, it has come to refer to the lessening of cold war tensions between the United States and the Soviet Union in the late 1960s and 1970s. Global instability encouraged both superpowers to limit the nuclear arms race, which formed the basis for the détente.

devshirme The tribute of male children that the Ottoman Turks took from their Christian subjects in the Balkans, the Ottoman Empire's holdings in southeastern Europe. The boys were removed from their homes, taught Turkish, usually converted to Islam, and trained for service in the civil administration or in the elite Janissary infantry corps. *See also* Janissary corps.

dharma In Hindu belief, performance of the duties appropriate to an individual's caste, with the understanding that good performance will lead to rebirth in a higher caste. In Buddhism, dharma refers to the teachings of the Buddha; in Jainism, it refers to moral virtue.

dhimmi From the Arabic for "people of the book" (that is, the Bible); Jews, Christians, and Zoroastrians in the Arab world who were permitted to practice their own religion as long as they paid a tax called the *jizya*. Arabs were actively seeking converts to Islam by the middle of the eighth century but did not force these "protected subjects" to convert.

dhow A ship with one or two lateen sails, developed by the Arabs and used along the coasts of the Arabian Peninsula, India, and East Africa in the trade of both goods and slaves.

diaspora A dispersion of people from their homeland. Although other cultures have experienced diasporas, the term has come to refer most often to the expulsion of the Jews from their homeland in ancient Israel. Many were taken by the Assyrians (722 B.C.E.) and neo-Babylonians (586 B.C.E.), though Jewish cultural and religious traditions were preserved in exile. Other Jewish diasporas occurred throughout history, notably after Jews rebelled against Rome in the first and second centuries C.E. The Atlantic slave trade created an African diaspora throughout Europe and the Americas.

divination The practice of seeking information on the future through various magical sources. Chinese kings of the Shang dynasty (ca. 1500–1050 B.C.E.) sought guidance from their ancestors by interpreting the cracks in heated cattle bones or tortoise shells.

divine right of kings The doctrine that kings were established in their rule by God and were accountable only to God. In such a system, the will of God and that of the king became inseparable. *See also* absolutism.

diwan An administrative organ that registered all Muslim soldiers in the early Islamic world, collected the taxes for their salaries, and financed charitable and public works undertaken by the caliph.

dual revolution The term used by historian Eric Hobsbawm to describe the fusion, beginning in 1815, of political and economic changes in Europe caused by England's Industrial Revolution of the late eighteenth century and the French Revolution (1789–1799). The two revolutions reinforced each other and led to new political ideologies such as liberalism and socialism.

Duma The elected representative assembly grudgingly created in Russia by Tsar Nicholas II (r. 1894–1917) in response to the 1905 revolution. When the Duma disagreed with the tsar, however, Nicholas II dissolved the assembly and changed the electoral laws to favor the nobility.

Dutch East India Company A joint stock company chartered in 1602 by the States General of the Netherlands, initially with the objective of taking the spice trade away from the Portuguese. Its broader purpose was to expand trade and promote relations between the Dutch government and its colonial ventures.

dynastic cycle The theory that Chinese dynasties rise and fall in a cyclical fashion. Failed dynasties were said to have lost the Mandate of Heaven and thus the right to govern. *See also* Mandate of Heaven.

dynasty A succession of rulers from the same family.

E

Eastern Orthodoxy A branch of Christianity that developed in the eastern part of the Roman Empire and gradually separated, mostly on matters of practice, from what became Roman Catholic Christianity in Western Europe. In 1054, representatives from the eastern and western branches mutually excommunicated each other in what is known as the Great Schism. Eastern Orthodoxy is noted for the subordination of the Church to political authorities, a clergy allowed to marry, the use of leavened bread in the Eucharist, and insistence on church councils as the ultimate authority in Christian belief and practice.

economic imperialism The practice whereby businesses from developed nations establish a commercial presence in Third World regions—sometimes colonies or former colonies of the wealthier nations—with the intent of making substantial profits.

economic nationalism The idea that countries should protect and foster their own businesses by imposing high protective tariffs on imported goods as well as eliminating tariffs within the country. Economic nationalism was first made popular by German thinker Friedrich List in the 1830s and 1840s; many Latin American countries embraced the idea in the twentieth century.

Edict of Nantes A law signed in 1598 by King Henry IV (r. 1589–1610) of France that ended decades of religious conflict by granting French Protestants limited religious freedoms and toleration. This shift in royal policy represented a significant trend in which the interests of the state prevailed over all other concerns, including religious ideals. The Edict remained in effect until revoked by Louis XIV (r. 1643–1715) in 1685.

EEC *See* European Economic Community.

Eightfold Path The code of conduct and spiritual practice, set forth by Buddha in his first sermon, that would allow his followers to achieve freedom from pain, anxiety, and suffering. *See also* Buddhism.

emir An Arab governor who was appointed and given overall responsibility for good order, maintenance of the armed forces, and tax collecting in conquered lands. Emirs allowed native officials to remain in office so that there was continuity with previous administrations.

empiricism A philosophical doctrine that emphasized the role of observation, experimentation, and deductive reasoning in the acquisition of knowledge. Although this approach to knowledge dates back to philosophers such as Aristotle (384–322 B.C.E.), in its modern sense, it is associated with the scientific method developed by seventeenth-century intellectuals Francis Bacon (1561–1626) of England and René Descartes (1596–1650) of France. Empiricism represented a significant turn from traditional thinking with its reliance on classical philosophy and the Scriptures.

enclosure movement A process in eighteenth-century England by which wealthy landowners consolidated their holdings by pressuring small farmers to sell their land or give up grazing rights on common lands. As a result, the English peasant class effectively disappeared, replaced by a more hierarchical rural society with wealthy landlords at the top, tenant farmers in the middle, and poor laborers at the bottom.

encomienda system In the Americas, the Crown-given right that allowed sixteenth-century Spanish conquerors to employ groups of Amerindians as agricultural or mining laborers or as tribute payers. In the Philippines, the encomienda system gave Spanish colonists the exclusive right to control public affairs and collect taxes in a specific locality.

endogamy Marriage that takes place within a defined group, such as a village or a kinship network.

enlightened absolutism The doctrine emerging from the eighteenth-century Enlightenment, which maintained that although the authority of the monarch is hereditary and absolute, the monarch is under obligation to rule with tolerance and compassion, in the best interest of his or her people.

Enlightenment The eighteenth-century intellectual movement whose proponents believed that political, social, and economic problems could be solved, and indefinite progress achieved, through the application of reason, education, and critical thinking. Based on the popularization of scientific discoveries and increased literacy, the Enlightenment often challenged religious and secular authorities by questioning traditional knowledge and the status quo.

environmentalism A movement begun in the mid-twentieth century that sought to preserve the natural world from the effects of human impact and to restore those areas already affected.

Epic of Gilgamesh A long poem written around 2500 B.C.E. about the adventures of the hero Gilgamesh. Written in cuneiform (a method of writing developed by the Sumerians around 3500 B.C.E.), it tells the story of King Gilgamesh and his search for immortality. A later version includes a description of a great flood that covered the earth, foreshadowing the biblical account of Noah's Ark. The version that exists today is a combination of many variations of the original tale.

Epicureanism A Greek system of philosophy, founded on the teachings of Epicurus (341–271 B.C.E.), which emphasized that a life of contentment, free from fear and suffering, was the greatest good. Epicurus's definition of pleasure referred to the "absence of disturbance." This meant that people should lead a sober life spent with friends and separated from daily distractions of turbulence, passions, and ordinary desires. He challenged traditional notions of Greek citizenship by allowing women and slaves to study in his group and by embracing women's participation in public and religious cults.

Esoteric Buddhism A sect of Buddhism that maintains that teachings containing the secrets of enlightenment have been secretly transmitted from the Buddha and can be accessed through initiation into the mandalas (cosmic diagrams), mudras (gestures), and mantras (verbal formulas).

Estates General A body of deputies representing the three estates, or orders, of France: the clergy (First Estate), the nobility (Second Estate), and everyone else (Third Estate). The Estates General originated in the fourteenth century as an advisory body but fell out of use after 1614 when the French monarchy adopted a more absolutist style of rule. A fiscal crisis forced Louis XVI (r. 1774–1792) to summon the Estates in 1789, and disputes about procedures of voting in this body paved the way to the French Revolution (1789–1799).

ethnogenesis The process by which new ethnic identities are created.

EU *See* European Union.

Eucharist A Christian sacrament in which the death of Christ is communally remembered through a meal of bread (representing Christ's body) and wine (representing Christ's blood). Catholics believe that the bread and wine turn into the blood and body of Christ upon consecration—a process called transubstantiation.

eunuch A castrated male who played an important role as a palace servant. Eunuchs were usually purchased as slaves and were often used to guard the ruler's harem of wives, concubines, female relatives, and children.

European Economic Community (EEC) Also known as the Common Market, an alliance formed by Italy, France, West Germany, Belgium, the Netherlands, and Luxembourg in 1957 and dedicated to developing common trade policies and reduced tariffs. It gradually developed into the European Union.

European Union (EU) The final step in a series of arrangements to increase political and economic cooperation between European states in the wake of World War II (1939–1945). It evolved from the European Economic Community (EEC or Common Market) formed in 1957. The EU was formally established in 1994, and twelve of its members adopted a common currency, the euro, in 2002.

evolution The scientific theory that life took shape over millions of years and that human life was not the result of divine creation but of a slow and changing biological process. It meant that human beings evolved or developed from animal species, ultimately apes. At its core, the theory embraced the concept of "natural selection," arguing that human life emerged from lower forms through a primal struggle for survival where some species were able to adapt and others died off. Although ideas of evolutionary change predate British scientist Charles Darwin, the publication of his *On the Origin of Species* in 1859 placed the issue at the forefront of political and scientific debate.

examination system *See* civil service examination.

exile A situation in which a person is forced to live outside his or her homeland. In the history of ancient Judah, the term refers to the period when the Babylonians deported the Judeans and settled them in Babylonia (ca. 587–530 B.C.E.). *See also* diaspora.

existentialism A literary and philosophical movement popular after World War II (1939–1945) that explored the meaning (or lack of meaning) of human existence in a world where evil seemed to triumph and God seemed absent. Existentialists addressed the question of "being," arguing that God did not endow spiritual goodness or determine the nature of a person's existence, but rather that the individual, through action and choice, created his or her authentic self.

experimental method The approach, first developed by astronomer Galileo Galilei in the seventeenth century, that the proper way to explore the workings of the universe was through repeatable experiments rather than speculation.

expressionism An artistic style rooted in impressionism that rejected realistic representations and instead tried to depict moods and emotions with abstract images. *See also* impressionism.

extraterritoriality A clause in the Treaty of Nanjing (1842), which ended the first Opium War (1839–1842), that made British subjects in China answerable only to British law. *See also* Opium Wars.

F

Factory Act of 1833 An act passed in England that limited the factory workday for children between nine and thirteen years of age to eight hours and that of adolescents between fourteen and eighteen years of age to twelve hours.

family economy An economic system in which production was directed toward family or community needs rather than toward sale for a distant market.

fascism A political movement that began in Italy in the 1920s under the leadership of Benito Mussolini (r. 1922–1945). Fascism glorified the state over the people and their individual or civil rights and stressed the importance of violence and warfare in making nations strong. It was characterized by extreme, often expansionist nationalism, an antisocialism aimed at destroying working-class movements, alliances with powerful capitalists and landowners, a dynamic and violent leader, and glorification of war and the military.

fatwa A legal opinion, informed by religious law, as issued by a judge in an Islamic court.

fealty An expression of allegiance to a higher political authority, often verified by swearing an oath of loyalty, giving tribute, and other gestures of submission.

federation A joining together of equal and self-governing states rather than a thoroughly unified nation.

feminism A movement seeking social and political equality for women with men. While it first emerged in nineteenth-century Europe and the United States, it achieved a global presence by the second half of the twentieth century. Along with seeking complete gender equity in the workplace and an end to discrimination, many feminists also argued for women's right to control their bodies via access to birth control and safe and legal abortions, as well as opposing the use of physiological differences to block women from opportunities in employment, education, and sports.

Fertile Crescent The geographic region in southwestern Asia that stretches in an arc from present-day Israel across Syria to southern Iraq along the Tigris and Euphrates rivers. The region's name indicates its ideal combination of soil, water, and temperature, which facilitates the growth of crops for food. The development of agriculture and the domestication of animals took place in the Fertile Crescent between 10,000–8000 B.C.E.; it was home to several early civilizations and the first large cities.

feudalism A term used by some historians to explain the social, economic, and political hierarchy that developed in Western Europe during the eighth century. Historians disagree on its precise usage: some use it to describe an economy of peasants dominated by nobility, while others define it as a relationship of obligation between lord and vassal. China and Japan arguably had unique versions of a feudal system, though the idea is controversial among scholars.

fief A portion of land, the use of which was given by a lord to a vassal in exchange for the latter's oath of loyalty. *See also* feudalism.

Final Solution *See* Holocaust.

Five Good Emperors Five of the most successful emperors in Roman history. The reign of Nerva (96–98 C.E.), Trajan (98–117 C.E.), Hadrian (117–138 C.E.), Antoninus Pius (138–161 C.E.), and Marcus Aurelius (161–180 C.E.) is often regarded by historians as a "Golden Age" of Roman history, marked by peaceful transfers of imperial power, prosperity, and strong economic and population growth.

Five Pillars of Islam The basic tenets of the Islamic faith, which include reciting a profession of faith in God and in Muhammad (ca. 570–632 C.E.) as God's prophet; prayer five times daily; fasting and prayer during the month of Ramadan; a pilgrimage to Mecca once in one's lifetime; and contribution of alms to the poor.

five-year plan An economic prospectus for comprehensive industrial and agricultural development under state control in Communist countries, such as the Soviet Union and China. Similar, though less extensive planning efforts have been undertaken in many countries.

Flores Man A recently discovered hominid species of Indonesia, noted for its small stature (just over three feet tall) and small brain. Archeologists estimate that it lived about 12,000 years ago.

foot binding The Chinese practice of tightly wrapping girls' feet to keep them from growing and to make the foot narrow and arched. An emphasis on small size and delicacy was central to views of female beauty; at first it was an elite practice, but later spread to all classes.

Forum A public area in the center of Rome that served as focal point of the political, spiritual, and economic life of the city, similar to a Greek agora.

Four Noble Truths The Buddha's message that pain and suffering are inescapable parts of life; suffering and anxiety are caused by human desires and attachments; people can understand and triumph over these weaknesses; and the triumph is made possible by following a simple code of conduct and spiritual practice, the Eightfold Path. *See also* Buddhism, Eightfold Path.

Fourteen Points A proposal by U.S. president Woodrow Wilson (r. 1913–1921) for the negotiation of peace during World War I (1914–1918). Wilson called for open diplomacy, arms reduction, flexibility in resolving colonial issues, and the self-determination of peoples. Although Wilson's views were popular in Europe, his vision largely failed.

Franco-Prussian War A war between France and Prussia in 1870 and 1871, in which France was quickly beaten by the newly modernized Prussian army. The war demonstrated the importance of new technologies, such as the train and the telegraph, which the Prussians used to their advantage. The quick defeat signaled a shift in power relations in Europe and was a key moment in the unification of Germany.

free trade A system in which the exchange of goods and services goes unrestricted by government tariffs, taxes, or other regulations.

French Revolution A massive and violent upheaval of French society (1789–1799) that overthrew the monarchy, sharply curtailed the influence of the French aristocracy, launched the "Terror" against the revolution's opponents, attacked the Catholic Church, and introduced a range of individual liberties as outlined in the Declaration of the Rights of Man and Citizen. *See also* Declaration of the Rights of Man and Citizen, Terror (France).

functionalism The principle that buildings, like industrial products, should serve the purpose for which they were made as well as possible. Functionalism was the driving force behind the modernist revolution in architecture that occurred in the late nineteenth and early twentieth centuries.

fundamentalism Occurring within all the major world religions, fundamentalism is a self-proclaimed return to the "fundamentals" of a religion and is marked by a militant piety and exclusivism.

G

galley A long, narrow ship propelled primarily by oars that was the main form of sea transportation in the Mediterranean world from ancient times through the seventeenth century. Galleys required vast crews of rowers, who were often prisoners of war, convicts, or slaves.

gathering and hunting peoples People who lived by collecting food rather than deliberately producing it. These people were also known as Paleolithic people, for their use of stone tools. This kind of economy sustained humankind for 95 percent or more of human history. *See also* Paleolithic era.

gazi *See* ghazi.

geisha A courtesan trained in the arts of singing, dancing, and conversation who entertained wealthy Japanese men. Desperately poor parents sometimes sold their young daughters to entertainment houses; the most attractive and talented of these were trained to be geisha.

General Assembly The second main body of the United Nations, first convened in 1946, in which every "peace-loving" state is eligible to join and participate. Each member has one vote, no matter its size, but General Assembly resolutions can become legally binding only if they are approved by all five permanent members of the Security Council (China, Russia, France, the United Kingdom, and the United States). *See also* Security Council.

general will A political concept, first set forth by French philosopher Jean-Jacques Rousseau (1712–1778), that refers to the desires or interest of the people as a whole, particularly in reference to their long-term needs. The general will is not necessarily set by the majority, however; a minority who can consider the people's future needs may also determine it.

Geneva Conference A meeting held in Switzerland in 1954 to restore peace within Korea and French Indochina, which was granted independence from France as the country of Vietnam.

gens de couleur libres French for "free people of color"; the freed slaves and people of mixed racial background in the French Caribbean colony of Saint-Domingue. They sought the same political rights as white Frenchmen and often owned slaves themselves before the revolutions that freed the slaves and created the Republic of Haiti in 1804.

germ theory The idea that disease was spread through filth containing harmful microorganisms, rather than by spontaneous generation. Although many earlier thinkers had supported variations of this idea, the modern germ theory is associated with Louis Pasteur (1822–1895), a French chemist who demonstrated that germs could be suppressed by heating a liquid—a process later called pasteurization.

ghazi Arabic for "holy warrior"; in Islam, a fighter who declares war against nonbelievers. In the mid-tenth century, Turks who converted to Islam often became ghazi and raided communities of unconverted Turks to take as slaves.

gladiators Criminals and convicts who fought in the Roman arena as public entertainment. Originally part of extravagant funeral shows, gladiators became popular entertainment for large Roman audiences under the rule of Augustus (r. 27 B.C.E.–14 C.E.). War captives, criminals, slaves, and free volunteers, gladiators were often wounded in their theatrical combat but rarely killed. Victory brought riches and celebrity but not social respectability.

glasnost Russian for "openness" or "publicity"; a policy instituted in the late 1980s by Soviet premier Mikhail Gorbachev (r. 1985–1991) calling for greater openness in speech and in thinking, which allowed greater cultural and intellectual freedom and ended most censorship of the media. The result was a burst of awareness of the problems and corruption of the Soviet system. *See also* perestroika.

global warming The belief among the majority of the world's scientists that hydrocarbons produced through the burning of fossil fuels and excessive deforestation have caused a greenhouse effect, trapping heat in the atmosphere and increasing global temperatures over time.

globalization The increasingly interconnected nature of the world's various peoples and societies in terms of politics, economics, and culture. Though globalization began as early as the sixteenth century, it achieved its greatest impact in the late twentieth and early twenty-first centuries.

glyph A figurative symbol, usually carved in stone, that renders an aspect of one of the ancient languages of Mesoamerica, either an entire word or a syllable.

Golden Horde The khanate that formed the western part of the Mongol Empire from around 1241 to 1480 in what is now south-central Russia. The Mongols did not occupy Russia as they had China and Persia and therefore had an uneven impact there. Russian princes could continue to rule as long as they paid homage and tribute to the Mongol khan, or leader. The Russian church was tolerated and exempted from taxes. *See also* khanate, Mongol Yoke.

Gothic An architectural style, originating in France in the twelfth century, that was characterized by pointed arches, ribbed vaults, and large stained-glass windows. Gothic architecture is marked by an emphasis on space and light: exteriors are often dark and forbidding, but the interiors represent lightness, harmony, and order. By the thirteenth century, Gothic architecture had spread from France to other European countries. In the late eighteenth and early nineteenth centuries, a revival of Gothic art, architecture, and literature looked to the Middle Ages for inspiration.

Great Depression The worldwide economic contraction that followed the stock market crash in the United States in 1929 as international trade dropped sharply, banks failed, and unemployment soared. With serious effects in industrialized and colonial economies alike, the international scope of the Great Depression illustrated the connectedness of the global economic system.

Great Khan A Turkish title meaning "lord of the steppe"; its bearer was the equivalent of an emperor. The Great Khan of the Mongols was chosen by the quriltai (council) of Mongol chiefs. The title is commonly associated with Chinggis (Genghis) Khan (r. 1206–1227).

Great Leap Forward A major Chinese initiative (1958–1960) led by Mao Zedong (r. 1949–1976) that was intended to promote rapid economic growth and collective living arrangements through large agricultural units called communes, small-scale industrialization in the rural areas, and broader knowledge of modern technology among ordinary people. Such policies gave rise to a massive economic crisis, widespread famine, and starvation, exacerbated by several years of poor weather.

Great Mutiny *See* Indian Rebellion.

Great Proletarian Cultural Revolution *See* Cultural Revolution.

Great Purges   Also called the Terror, the Great Purges of the late 1930s were a massive attempt to cleanse the Soviet Union of supposed "enemies of the people." Nearly a million people were executed between 1936 and 1941, and between 4 and 5 million more were sentenced to forced labor in the gulag. *See also* gulag.

Great Schism   A term referring to one of two different ruptures in the history of the Christian church. The first came to a head in 1054 between the Roman Catholic Church and the Eastern Orthodox Church after centuries of tension between them. The second, from 1378 to 1417, was when the Catholic Church had two rival claimants to the papacy: one in Rome, Italy, and the other in Avignon, France. The European powers sided with one or the other depending on their political ties, and the Schism weakened the religious faith of many Christians. *See also* Catholicism, Eastern Orthodoxy.

Great Wall   A rammed-earth fortification along the northern border of China, built and rebuilt over many centuries beginning around 500 B.C.E. Intended to prevent the penetration into China of nomadic peoples considered "barbarians" by the Chinese, it involved the forced labor of hundreds of thousands of subjects.

Great War   *See* World War I.

Greco-Persian Wars   A period of warfare (499–479 B.C.E) between the Greeks and the Persians, including two major Persian invasions of Greece (490 B.C.E. and 480 B.C.E.) in which the Persians were defeated on both land and sea.

Greek fire   A potent military weapon of the Byzantine navy used in the mid-eighth century, comprised of a combustible oil that floated on water and burst into flames when it hit its target. The weapon was responsible for many Byzantine naval victories and enabled the endurance of the Byzantine Empire (330–1453).

Green Revolution   An increase in developing nations' food production, beginning in the 1950s, that stemmed from the introduction of high-yielding wheats, hybrid seeds, chemical fertilizers, and other agricultural advancements.

guild   An association of craftspeople, merchants, or professionals that operated variously in many civilizations during the pre-industrial era. In Europe by the second half of the twelfth century, guilds became professional associations defined by rules that regulated, protected, and policed their membership. A child began as an apprentice, placed into the tutelage of a master for a number of years to learn a craft. This was followed by the rank of journeyman, who worked for a master for a wage. The final rank was master, or craftsman, who owned his own shop and dominated the offices and policies of the guild.

gulag A network of Soviet prison/labor camps established in the early twentieth century across the country. The term was derived from an acronym for the administrative arm of the government that ran the camps. Housing millions of prisoners under often lethal conditions, the gulag contained and punished those seen as dissidents or threats to the state and provided an involuntary labor force for economic development projects in remote regions such as Siberia. The gulag grew to its greatest extent during the Great Purges under the leadership of Joseph Stalin, who held power in the Soviet Union between 1929 and 1953.

gunboat diplomacy The signing of treaties and agreements under threat of military violence, such as the opening of Japan to U.S. trade in 1853 after Commodore Matthew Perry's demands.

H

hadith A collection of the sayings of or anecdotes about Muhammad (ca. 570–632 C.E.) and his immediate followers. Hadiths rank second only to the Quran as a source of Islamic law.

Haitian Revolution A series of uprisings (1791–1804) of slaves and free blacks in the French Caribbean colony of Saint-Domingue and the only fully successful slave rebellion in world history. It was sparked by the French Revolution (1789–1799) and led to the establishment of the independent state of Haiti.

hajj The pilgrimage to Mecca that every Muslim who is able is required to make. It is one of the Five Pillars of Islam.

Hanseatic League A trade alliance between major cities and small towns along the Baltic and North Seas that formed in the thirteenth century. The Hanseatic League was centered in Lübeck, Germany, and had almost total control over trade in the Baltic and North Seas; however, it went into decline in the sixteenth and seventeenth centuries, as it was eclipsed in the region by the English, Dutch, and Swedes.

harem The separate quarters of a Muslim house or palace where women lived. It could contain not only wives and concubines but also mothers, sisters, aunts, and children of the head of the household as well.

Hebrew Bible The sacred books—in prose and poetry—that document the monotheistic religious ideas of the peoples of Israel and Judah, their views on history, law, and the relationship with god Yahweh.

Hebrews A Middle Eastern people whose development of a monotheistic faith provided the foundation of modern Judaism, Christianity, and Islam. Their traditions describe their early migration from Mesopotamia to Palestine, the enslavement of some in Egypt, and their escape back to Palestine. There they established a state around 1000 B.C.E., which soon split into two parts, Israel and Judah. These states were later incorporated into the Roman Empire.

Heian period The period of Japanese history from 794 to 1192 C.E. during which life centered around Japan's second capital city, Heian (now known as Kyoto), which was modeled on the Chinese capital of Chang'an. It saw the rise of an aristocratic culture, the development of a Japanese writing system, and new schools of Buddhism.

heliocentric theory The theory that the earth and other planets revolve around the sun, proposed by Polish astronomer Nicolaus Copernicus (1473–1543) and accepted in the West in the sixteenth century. Although heliocentric hypotheses were first put forth by ancient Greek philosophers, most people continued to believe that the sun and planets revolved around the earth. The heliocentric theory was originally condemned by the Catholic Church for contradicting the notion that the earth was the center of God's creation, a key component of biblical accounts of creation.

Hellenistic era The period from 323 to 30 B.C.E. in which Greek culture spread widely throughout the Eurasian kingdoms ruled by the political successors of Alexander the Great (r. 336–323 B.C.E.).

helots A class of Greeks who were captured and forced into permanent servitude by Sparta. Most came from the region of Messenia, which Sparta vanquished around 700 B.C.E. Although they outnumbered free Spartans, the helots' slave-like status was maintained through beatings, public humiliation, and legally sanctioned violence. Possessing few rights, helots labored on farms and in households. The militarization of Spartan society developed to prevent rebellion among the helots.

heresy A religious belief or set of beliefs that differs from officially sanctioned dogma. In the Christian world, heresy was perceived as a threat not only to church authority but also to society in general, since it was believed that it could provoke God's anger. As the papacy grew in power during the high Middle Ages (ca. 1000–1200), new organizations and methods were devised to detect, prevent, and punish heresy; among these was the Inquisition. *See also* Inquisition.

Hidalgo-Morelos rebellion A socially radical peasant insurrection, driven by high food prices and demand for land that began in Mexico in 1810 and was led by the priests Miguel Hidalgo and José Morelos. The rebellion was put down by Creole landowners and the Catholic Church, but it did lead to Mexican independence in 1813.

hieroglyphics An ancient Egyptian form of writing that employed pictures or symbols as its characters. One of several scripts used by the Egyptian peoples, hieroglyphs were developed during the Old Kingdom period (ca. 3050–2190 B.C.E.) and used for official texts. Simplified scripts were later developed for everyday use.

hijra   Arabic for "migration"; the flight of Muhammad (ca. 570–632 C.E.) and his original seventy followers from Mecca to Yathrib (later Medina) in 622 C.E. The journey marks the starting point of the Islamic calendar. Medina offered to protect Muhammad from the hostility he had faced in Mecca; he found many willing converts there, and Islam began to thrive.

Hinayana Buddhism   *See* Theravada Buddhism.

Hinduism   The name given (first by Muslims) to the body of religious teachings and practices, derived from the Brahmanic religion of the Vedic era, that developed between 400 B.C.E. and 200 C.E. in response to the challenge of Buddhism. In practice, what outsiders called Hinduism was an enormously varied set of beliefs, rituals, practices, philosophies, and sects with no overall organizational structure. It provided many ways for practitioners to realize the ultimate goal of union with the divine source known as Brahma. Defined by Indian intellectuals as a distinctive and separate religious tradition in the nineteenth century, it is the main religious tradition of India today.

HIV   *See* acquired immunodeficiency syndrome.

Holocaust   The Nazi genocide of 6 million Jews and many more "undesirables" in German-occupied lands during World War II (1939–1945). Victims were murdered in mass pogroms, worked and starved to death in forced labor camps, and executed in death camps as part of Adolf Hitler's "Final Solution," his plan to exterminate all of the Jews in Europe.

Holy Alliance   An alliance formed by Austria, Russia, and Prussia in September 1815 against the ideas and politics of the French Revolution (1789–1799). It became a symbol of the repression of liberal and revolutionary movements all over Europe.

hominid   The biological family that includes modern humans and their various bipedal (walking on two feet) ancestors.

Homo erectus   A species of hominid who lived in Asia from around 1 million years ago to perhaps 50,000 years ago.

Homo sapiens   The species of hominid to which modern humans belong. Most scholars place the origin of *Homo sapiens* in Africa perhaps 200,000 years ago. Emerging out of Africa about 100,000 years ago, they gradually migrated to the rest of the world.

hoplites Heavily armed soldiers of the Greek infantry. Originating around the eighth century B.C.E., hoplites were citizens who constituted the main strike force of a city-state's militia. Hoplites fought in a phalanx—a solid block of soldiers set up in rows of up to sixteen men that could charge through enemy ranks. Hoplites had to provide their own expensive arms and armor; thus, the hoplite ranks were open only to wealthier citizens.

House of Wisdom An academic center for research and translation of foreign texts that was established in Baghdad in 830 C.E. by the Abbasid caliph al-Mamun.

Huguenots The name given to Protestants in France in the mid-sixteenth century. Often severely persecuted, they were granted a reluctant toleration by the Edict of Nantes in 1598 following a long period of religious warfare. *See also* Edict of Nantes.

human sacrifice A widely practiced religious rite, particularly prominent in Mesoamerican religion. Sacrificial victims, often war captives, were slain on an altar as a means of paying debts to the gods and thereby ensuring the continuance of human life.

humanism A literary and intellectual movement that arose in Italy during the early fifteenth century to elevate the writings of Greco-Roman antiquity and to reconcile classical learning with Christianity. It was so named because its practitioners studied or supported the liberal arts—grammar, rhetoric, poetry, history, and moral philosophy—or humanities. Humanism spread to northern Europe in the late fifteenth and early sixteenth centuries and provided the foundations for the European Renaissance.

Hundred Years' War A major conflict between France and England (1337–1453) over rival claims to territory in France. The two states' need to finance the war helped encourage their administrative development.

hunter-gatherers *See* gathering and hunting peoples.

I

Ice Age Any of a number of cold periods in the earth's history, the last of which reached its peak around 20,000 years ago. Colder climates in northern regions encouraged southward migration, and the consolidation of ocean water in polar ice caps created land bridges between previously unconnected regions.

iconoclasm Greek for "the breaking of icons"; the destruction of physical representations of religious figures, such as saints, the Virgin Mary, and Jesus. Byzantine emperors from 726 to 787 banned such icons and ordered them destroyed, a movement perhaps inspired by the Muslim prohibition against the worship of idols. Although icons had been an important feature of seventh-century Byzantine religious life, many people, including the emperor, believed they were prohibited by the Bible's injunction against graven images. During the Protestant Reformation, images of the saints, stained-glass windows, and paintings were destroyed by Calvinist Protestants on the same grounds. *See also* Calvinism, Protestant Reformation.

ideograph *See* logographic script.

imam In Shia Islam, the supreme leader of the religious community. The twelve imams of early Shia Islam were Muhammad's cousin and son-in-law Ali (r. 656–661 C.E.) and his descendants.

imperialism The aggressive effort of particular nations or peoples to dominate others. The term is often used to describe Western dominance of the non-West through economic exploitation and political rule, guided by economic interest and sometimes a sense of obligation to "civilize" native peoples. It is distinct from colonialism, which usually implied establishment of permanent settler communities.

impressionism A mid- to late-nineteenth-century artistic, and later musical, style in which the artist attempted to capture a single moment by focusing on the ever-changing light and color found in ordinary scenes. It was influenced by Japanese art and reacted against the realism of photographs. Impressionist painters used splotches, dots, and obvious brush strokes to convey mood.

indentured laborer An emigrant who agreed to work for a certain number of years, specified in a contract, in exchange for his or her passage. A rise in indentured labor stemmed from the abolition of the slave trade in the early nineteenth century; Indian laborers replaced black slaves in British colonies, and the Spanish government recruited Chinese to work their plantations in Cuba. Indentured laborers were usually treated little better than slaves and subjected to dangerous, grueling work.

Indian Civil Service The bureaucracy that administered the government of India under British colonial rule in the nineteenth century. Entry into its elite ranks was by Western-style examinations that Indians were eligible to take, but that were offered only in England.

Indian National Congress A predominantly Hindu organization dedicated to the rights of Indians and eventually the independence of India from British rule. It was founded in 1885 by members of the Western-educated Indian elite, but became a mass nationalist party under Mohandas Gandhi's leadership in the 1920s. For several decades it was the dominant political force following India's independence in 1947.

Indian Ocean commercial network The massive, interconnected web of commerce among the lands that bordered on the Indian Ocean. Beginning with the ancient civilizations of Mesopotamia and the Indus Valley, it eventually stretched from southern China to eastern Africa and included not only the exchange of luxury and bulk goods but also the exchange of ideas and crops. It was the world's largest sea-based system of communication and exchange before the network was badly disrupted by Portuguese intrusion beginning around 1500.

Indian Rebellion A revolt (1857–1858) by the Indian Army against Britain's expanding presence in India and its disregard for Indian autonomy and local beliefs. Indian soldiers, known as sepoys, conquered the old Mughul capital at Delhi and declared independence for India. Known by the British as the Great Mutiny or the Indian Mutiny, the rebellion was quickly put down and led the British to change their governing philosophy in the region. They ended the Mughul Empire, took control of the British East India Company, and implemented a policy of direct rule of India by the British government.

Indo-European A family of related languages, spoken from Europe to India, that probably originated in Turkey between 7000 and 3500 B.C.E. These languages, including Greek, Latin, Persian, Sanskrit (the sacred tongue of ancient India), and, much later, English share enough common words and grammatical forms to indicate that they descended from this early family of languages.

indulgence In Catholic practice, a remission of sins one can earn by performing good deeds or religious tasks to avoid purgatory after death. Widely used by the thirteenth century, the practice was based on the Catholic doctrine that Christ had given Saint Peter and his successors, the popes, the authority to lift the penalties for sin. As the practice of granting indulgences developed, they could be purchased for cash and became a lucrative source of income for the church, a practice that came under fire during the Protestant Reformation. *See also* Protestant Reformation.

Industrial Revolution A series of technological and organizational changes that included the steam engine and the factory system. It began in Great Britain in the 1770s and 1780s before spreading to much of Europe in the first half of the nineteenth century. Subsequently it became a global phenomenon. In its wake the Industrial Revolution brought more massive transformation to every aspect of human life than anything since the Agricultural Revolution. The Industrial Revolution was characterized by new methods of manufacturing, including machines capable of mass production. They, in turn, made possible the greater availability and affordability of consumer goods, rapid urbanization, changes in gender roles, and the rise of a new social class of laborers who worked in urban factories, displacing skilled artisans.

infidel A nonbeliever or outsider in respect to a particular faith. The notion has been particularly prominent in the Christian and Islamic worlds.

Inquisition A court of inquiry authorized by the Roman papacy that sought to ferret out and punish heretics and religious dissidents. Punishments varied: imprisonment—sometimes permanent—was the most common, but some accused were ordered to go on pilgrimages, wear crosses on their clothes, or be burned alive. The Spanish Inquisition of the fifteenth century particularly targeted Jews whom they suspected had not completely converted.

Investiture Conflict The confrontation between Pope Gregory VII (r. 1073–1085) and Holy Roman Emperor Henry IV (r. 1056–1105) over the right to appoint and install bishops. Each man believed that his office entitled him to lead the church and make all appointments. The struggle between Gregory and Henry led to intermittent war from 1077 to 1122, ultimately ending the secular leader's role in choosing churchmen and laying the foundation for the modern Western distinction between church and state.

Iranian Revolution The violent 1979 reaction to the Westernization and secularization of Iran. Islamic fundamentalists deposed the shah and sought to rebuild Iran into a true Islamic state.

Islam A religion based on the teachings of the prophet Muhammad (ca. 570–632 C.E.), contained in the Quran and believed to be a direct revelation from God. Its core teachings involve personal submission to Allah and the creation of a just society based on Islamic principles. The followers of Islam, called Muslims, are obligated to adhere to the Five Pillars of Islam, the basic tenets of the faith. *See also* Five Pillars of Islam.

Islamic revivalism A large number of movements in Islamic lands that promote a return to the Quran (sacred scripture) and the sharia (Islamic law) as a guide to public as well as private life, often in opposition to key elements of Western secular culture.

J

Jainism A religion founded in India in the sixth century B.C.E. by Vardhamana Mahavira, who believed that all creatures, even plants and inanimate objects, had souls. He encouraged his followers to practice asceticism (denial of bodily comforts and rejection of property) and nonviolence.

Janissary corps Christian slave children and war captives who were raised by the Ottoman sultan as Muslims and served in the army from the fourteenth to the nineteenth century. An elite military unit, they trained under strict codes of discipline and ultimately gained power within the Ottoman Empire (Turkey); many officials of the Ottoman bureaucracy were once members of the corps. The rank of Janissary was so desirable that by the seventeenth century, membership was only through inheritance, although some Muslims did attempt to join by bribery.

Japan, Inc. A nickname developed in the 1980s to describe the intricate relationship that existed between the business world of Japan and its government. Some Americans and Europeans believed that this collusion gave the Japanese an unfair trading advantage and urged their own governments to retaliate.

jati A caste or division of Indian society that identifies an individual's occupation and social standing. *See also* caste system.

Java War The 1825–1830 war between the Dutch government and the Javanese, fought over the extension of Dutch control of the island.

jihad Arabic for "struggle"; a term for both the spiritual striving of each Muslim toward a godly life and armed struggle against the forces of unbelief and evil that threaten Islam.

jizya A special tax paid by dhimmis, or non-Muslims, in Muslim-ruled territory in return for freedom to practice their own religion. *See also* dhimmi.

Judaism The monotheistic religion developed by the Hebrew people, emphasizing a sole personal god (Yahweh) who transcended the world he created but who also showed compassion for the poor and marginalized. The Jews came to understand their relationship to Yahweh as a covenant, and in exchange for their devotion and obedience, Yahweh would bless and protect them as his chosen people. *See also* Hebrew Bible, Hebrews.

junk A ship first built in China in the second century B.C.E. with square sails; it was developed into an ocean-worthy vessel and enabled Chinese trade and exploration.

K

Kaaba A black cube-shaped stone structure in Mecca. Originally it housed the various "idols" of pre-Islamic Arabian religion. Rededicated by Muhammad (ca. 570–632 C.E.) as the central shrine of the new Islamic faith, it is the goal of Muslims on a pilgrimage or hajj.

kabuki A form of Japanese theater that originated in 1603 and featured crude stories of love and romance, elaborate costumes and makeup, song, dance, and poetry. Kabuki was originally performed by women, but they were banned from the stage in 1629 on the premise that they compromised public morals; male actors continued the tradition of seductive performances.

kami Sacred spirits of Japan associated with human ancestors and natural phenomena. Numerous kami were integrated into Japanese Buddhism as local representatives of Buddhist deities or principles. The worship of kami was much later called Shinto.

kamikaze The "divine wind" that the Japanese claimed saved them from attack by Mongol forces in 1281. The name was later given to the Japanese aviators in World War II (1939–1945) who crashed their planes into U.S. naval ships.

karma In traditional Indian belief, the tally of good and bad deeds that determines the status of an individual's next life.

keiretsu In Japan, a conglomeration of financial or industrial institutions strengthened by shareholding connections and mutually beneficial relationships. They appeared in the years following World War II (1939–1945) and took the place of the family-run *zaibatsu*, which were eliminated in 1940. *See also* zaibatsu.

khanate The four units into which the Mongol Empire was divided after the death of Chinggis Khan (r. 1206–1227). One of Chinggis's lines of descent took leadership of each khanate. *See also* Golden Horde.

khipu An intricate system of knotted and colored strings used by early Peruvian cultures to store information such as census and tax records.

kibbutz A Jewish collective farm on which each member shares equally in the work, rewards, and defense. Such forms of agricultural and industrial organization helped Jews in Palestine, who had come from many different countries, forge a cohesive community during the first half of the twentieth century. *See also* commune.

kiva A large room, sometimes underground, for meetings and religious ceremonies located at the center of the residential compounds in early societies of southwestern North America.

Korean War A civil war that broke out in 1950 and ended in 1953 in a stalemate. It was fought for control of the Korean peninsula between the Communist North Koreans and the anti-Communist South Koreans. The United States, seeking to prevent the spread of communism, intervened on the side of the South Koreans; Communist USSR and China backed the forces of the North.

Kristallnacht German for "crystal night"; the evening of November 9, 1938, when Nazi-led gangs burned and looted Jewish businesses, synagogues, and homes, killing ninety-one Jews and destroying over 7,500 businesses. The Nazi government then fined the Jewish community for this "Night of the Broken Glass" and ordered them to pay for the damage incurred during the riot.

Kshatriya The Indian social class of warriors and leaders of society, in rank second only to the Brahmin class of priests. *See also* caste system.

kulaks Prosperous landed peasants who were stripped of their land and livestock under Joseph Stalin (r. 1929–1953). Communists cast the kulaks as exploiters of the poor and began evicting them from their farms in the late 1920s, confiscating their grain to feed urban workers. They generally were not permitted to join the collective farms established by Stalin, and they themselves often starved or were deported to forced-labor camps.

Kyoto protocol An international agreement to reduce greenhouse gas emissions in an effort to slow global warming; as of November 2007, 174 countries had subscribed to the agreement, but the refusal by the United States to ratify the protocol has caused international tensions.

L

laissez-faire French for "let it be"; an economic doctrine that advocated freeing economies from government intervention and control. Developed by British economist Adam Smith in his work *An Inquiry into the Nature and Causes of the Wealth of Nations* (1776), this ideology resulted from the application of eighteenth-century Enlightenment principles of individual liberty to economics.

lateen sail A triangular-shaped sail that gives a ship greater maneuverability in varying wind directions. It was in use for thousands of years in the Indian Ocean and the Arab world as well as in the Mediterranean Sea and among Polynesian sailors in the Pacific. There remains some uncertainty as to precisely when and where it was first used and what influence Mediterranean and Indian Ocean sailmakers had on each other.

Lateran Accords A 1929 agreement that recognized the Vatican as a tiny independent state and made Catholicism Italy's national religion, with Benito Mussolini (r. 1922–1945) agreeing to give the church heavy financial support. In turn, the pope expressed his satisfaction and urged Italians to support Mussolini's fascist government.

latifundia Huge estates operated by slave labor that operated in parts of the Roman Empire, producing goods for export.

Latin American revolutions A series of uprisings in the Spanish and Portuguese colonies of Latin America (1810–1826) that established the independence of new states from colonial rule. However, the new governments that were created still excluded much of the population, and local elites took over the exploitation of the peasantry from colonial elites. *See also* Creoles.

law code of Hammurabi A proclamation issued by the Babylonian king Hammurabi (r. 1792–1750 B.C.E.) "to establish law and justice in the language of the land, thereby prompting the welfare of the people." Although it called for harsh punishments, it is pervaded with a spirit of justice and a sense of responsibility. However, it maintained that there were fundamental distinctions between men and women and people of different classes.

League of Nations The international organization established following World War I (1914–1918) to maintain peace by arbitrating disputes and promoting collective security. It was ultimately an ineffectual body, hampered in part by the United States' lack of participation, despite the fact that the league had been the vision of President Woodrow Wilson (r. 1913–1921). It dissolved in 1946 and was succeeded by the United Nations. *See also* United Nations.

Legalism A Chinese political philosophy distinguished by an adherence to clear laws with vigorous punishments. Legalists maintained that only the state and its ruler could act in the long-term interests of the people; they laid the basis for China's later bureaucratic government.

levée en masse French for "rise together"; specifically, the call to military service issued by the revolutionary government of France in 1793. The sentiment echoed and impacted the growth of nationalism in other countries and colonies. *See also* Atlantic revolutions.

li *See* qi.

liberalism An economic and political ideology that emphasizes free trade, representative government, laws to protect freedoms, and individual rights, such as freedom of speech and religion, as the best means for promoting social and economic improvement.

liberation theology A twentieth- and twenty-first-century Christian movement in Latin America and elsewhere, particularly among Catholics, that argues the need for Christians to engage in the pursuit of social justice and human rights. It combines some elements of Marxism with Catholic theology.

Linear A The administrative writing system of the Minoans, used until the fifteenth century B.C.E., which has still not been fully deciphered.

Linear B The administrative writing system of the Mycenaeans, used to record an early form of the Greek language (ca. 1800–1300 B.C.E.).

Little Ice Age A period of prolonged cool weather in the temperate zones of the earth that had adverse effects on agricultural production and resulted in famine in some places. Dating is uncertain, but many scholars place it between the sixteenth and early nineteenth centuries.

loess Deposited by wind, soil that is fertile and easy to work. It is the dominant soil in China and enabled early Chinese civilizations to grow crops effectively.

logographic script A language in which each word is represented by a single symbol, as in Chinese. The many years of study necessary to master the reading and writing of the Chinese script added to the prestige of education.

Long March The 6,000-mile retreat of the Chinese Communist army in 1934, under threat of extermination by the Nationalists, to a remote region on the northwestern border of China, during which tens of thousands lost their lives.

Lucknow Pact A 1916 alliance between the Muslim League and Hindus leading the Indian National Congress. It created a powerful united front of Hindus and Muslims as they sought to become a self-governing British dominion.

M

madrassa A formal college for higher instruction in the teachings of Islam as well as in religious law, grammar, rhetoric, and other subjects. Madrassas were established throughout the Islamic world beginning in the eleventh century. Often founded by a wealthy Muslim as a demonstration of his piety and charity, the madrassa was a key feature of Islamic education.

Mahayana Buddhism The popular development of Buddhism, beginning around 100 C.E. More than did traditional (Theravada) Buddhism, it viewed the Buddha as a divine figure, emphasized the power of the supernatural, and stressed the potential for laypersons to achieve enlightenment through the aid of various buddhas and bodhisattvas. *See also* bodhisattva.

malaria An infectious disease spread by mosquitoes, usually contracted in tropical areas with standing pools of water. The disease was frequently fatal for European colonizers, who did not have the natural immunity of Africans and native peoples of the Americas.

mamluk A slave soldier, originally of Turkish origin, recruited to serve in the army of Turkish sultans and employed to stave off power struggles. Mamluks were well paid, and many later gained high positions at the courts of the rulers they defended. They took control of Egypt from 1250 to 1517 and staffed their own armies with unconverted Turkish or Christian slaves.

Mandate of Heaven The Chinese theory that Heaven gives the emperor a mandate to rule only as long as he does so in the interests of the people. An emperor in ancient China was known as the Son of Heaven and wielded symbols of kingship believed to have been sent to Earth when the gods established monarchy.

mandate system The League of Nations covenant that granted the victors of World War I (1914–1918) in its membership—chiefly Britain and France, as well as South Africa, New Zealand, Australia and Japan—political control over Germany's former colonies, such as Togo, Cameroon, Syria, and Palestine. It continued the practice of carving up the globe into territories controlled by various European powers at a time when many of those countries were themselves weak and bankrupt. The mandate system aroused anger and resistance both in the territories themselves and among German citizens.

Manichaeism A religious tradition founded in third-century Persia that combined elements of Zoroastrianism, Christianity, and Buddhism.

manorialism The economic system that governed rural life in medieval Europe. A lord's manor—a large, organized estate consisting normally of arable fields, vineyards, meadows, and woodland—was worked by peasant families under his jurisdiction in exchange for his protection.

manumission The freeing of individual slaves by their masters. Manumission was a widespread practice in ancient Greece and enabled the former slaves to become citizens.

Marxism An economic and political philosophy predicting the collapse in revolution of industrial capitalist economies and their replacement by a socialist society. Devised by the philosopher and economist Karl Marx (1818–1883). Also called Marxian socialism, it formed the basis of socialist and Communist revolutions in the Soviet Union, China, Cuba, and elsewhere.

matriarchy An imaginary social order in which women dominate.

matrilineal society A society in which people trace ancestry and descent by the female side of the family. Many early societies of West Africa used a matrilineal system of descent, though some eventually shifted to a patrilineal system. *See also* patrilineal society.

May Fourth Movement A nationalist movement in China against foreign imperialists. It began on May 4, 1919, when Chinese students protested the decision of the Versailles Peace Conference to leave the Shandong Peninsula in the hands of Japan. *See also* Treaty of Versailles.

medical revolution A period from the late 1800s to after World War II (1939–1945) during which scientists discovered vaccines for many of the most deadly diseases. According to the World Health Organization, medical advances reduced deaths from smallpox, cholera, and plague by more than 95 percent worldwide between 1951 and 1966.

Meiji Restoration A change in the Japanese government in 1867–1868 that reinstalled the emperor as legitimate ruler in place of the military leader, or shogun, who had ruled for over two centuries. The goal of the Meiji (meaning "enlightened rule") Restoration was to establish Japan as a modern, technologically powerful state free from Western control. It inspired other regions in Asia and Africa to similarly resist the West.

mercantilism An economic theory based on the premise that a nation's power and wealth were determined by its supply of precious metals and arguing that governments should intervene to increase national wealth by any means, such as establishing overseas trading companies, granting manufacturing monopolies, and standardizing production methods.

mestizo A person of mixed ancestry in the Spanish colonies of the Americas, typically descended from a European father and a Native American mother. By 1800 they accounted for more than a quarter of the colonial population, with many aspiring to join the local elite.

Mexican Revolution Long and bloody war (1910–1920) in which Mexican reformers from the middle class joined with workers and peasants to overthrow the dictator Porfirio Díaz (r. 1876–1911) and create a new, much more democratic political order.

Middle Passage The name commonly given to the shipping of African slaves across the Atlantic to the Americas. Packed on board in inhumane conditions, an estimated 15 percent of slaves died during the journey.

Mississippian emergence The name given by scholars to the spread of common technologies, cultural practices, and forms of social and political organization among a wide range of farming societies in the Mississippi Valley of North America beginning in the eighth century and peaking in the eleventh to sixteenth centuries.

mita In the Inca Empire (1438–1533), a draft rotary system that determined when men of a particular region performed public works.

mixed economy An economy that combines elements of the market with state regulation.

modernization The process of obtaining the technological, economic, and social capacity to produce wealth characteristic of the early industrial societies of Europe and North America.

moksha In Hindu belief, liberation from the wheel of life and union with Brahma.

monarchy A type of government in which a king represents the community, theoretically reigning according to law and respecting the needs of the citizens. Monarchs often justified their right to rule by claiming that it was God's will. *See also* absolutism, divine right of kings, Mandate of Heaven.

monasticism A movement of Christian asceticism emphasizing the retreat from the everyday world to live a life of self-denial and prayer. Monasticism first emerged in Egypt in the second half of the third century but soon spread throughout the European and Mediterranean worlds. Known as monks, practitioners originally lived alone but gradually formed communities providing mutual support in the pursuit of holiness.

Mongol Yoke The 200-year rule of the Mongols over the territories of an emerging Russian state. Moscow was made the center of Mongol tribute collection and later served as the nucleus of the Russian state when Mongol domination receded in the fifteenth century. *See also* Golden Horde.

monotheism The belief in one god, which is a characteristic of Christianity, Judaism, and Islam. The Pharaoh Akhenaten (r. 1367–1350 B.C.E.), who forced the Egyptian people to worship a single deity named Aten, is believed by some historians to have been the first monotheist. *See also* polytheism.

monsoon An alternating wind current that blew eastward across the Indian Ocean in the summer and westward in the winter, facilitating India's trade with other maritime countries.

movable type A system of printing, employing reusable individual letters, that made the mass production of books and written materials possible at a lower cost. It was initially developed in China before the early thirteenth century but abandoned because it did not work well with the expansive Chinese script. Johannes Gutenberg (ca. 1400–1468) is credited with its development in Europe in the fifteenth century.

mulatto A person of mixed African and European ancestry.

multinational corporation A business that operates in a number of foreign countries by sending large segments of its manufacturing, finance, sales, and other business components abroad, often to Third World countries where labor costs are inexpensive. Beginning in the early twentieth century and expanding dramatically after World War II (1939–1945), multinational corporations have taken on increased importance since the late twentieth century with the rise of the global economy.

Muslim League The All-India Muslim League, created in 1906 as a response to the Indian National Congress in India's struggle for independence from Britain. The League's leader, Muhammad Ali Jinnah (1876–1948), argued that regions of India with a Muslim majority should form a separate state called Pakistan.

mystery religion A religious group whose secret rites involved prayers, hymns, ritual purification, sacrifices, and other forms of worship. Popular during the Golden Age of Athens (ca. 500–400 B.C.E.) and prevalent in the Roman Empire, mystery cults were connected with individual deities and centered on providing worshippers with divine protection and secret knowledge about the celestial and human worlds.

N

NAFTA *See* North American Free Trade Agreement.

Nahuatl The language of both the Toltecs and the Aztecs in Mesoamerica.

National Liberation Front The victorious anticolonial movement in Algeria, which won its independence from France in 1962.

nationalism A political ideology that holds that all people derive their identities from their nations, which are defined by shared language, tradition, customs, and history. Emerging in the early nineteenth century, nationalism fueled revolutions and posed a serious challenge to the rule of multiethnic empires such as the Ottoman Empire and the Austrian Empire. Nationalist competition helped fuel imperialism in the late nineteenth century, drove the world wars of the twentieth century, and undermined empires of all kinds. *See also* imperialism.

nation-state A sovereign political entity and defined territory of modern times representing a supposedly united people—joined by blood, culture, language, or common experience—instead of a collection of disparate cities or regions.

Native Land Act A 1913 South African law that limited black ownership of land to native reserves encompassing only one-seventh of the country and formed the foundation for apartheid. Poor, overpopulated, and too small to feed themselves, the rural native reserves served as a pool of cheap, temporary black labor for white farms, gold mines, and urban factories. *See also* apartheid.

NATO *See* North Atlantic Treaty Organization.

natural law The belief that the laws governing ethical behavior are written into nature itself and therefore possess universal validity.

natural philosophy The scientific study of nature. Based on the writings of Aristotle (384–322 B.C.E.), the term was used before the Scientific Revolution to designate the disciplines of astronomy, mathematics, and physics.

natural selection *See* evolution.

Nazism A movement that advocated a strongly authoritarian and nationalist regime based on notions of racial superiority. Adolf Hitler (r. 1933–1945) and the Nazi Party attempted to "purify" the German state by killing Jews and other "undesirables." *See also* Holocaust.

Neanderthaler A hominid species that inhabited Europe and Western Asia from 400,000 to between 30,000 and 25,000 years ago.

négritude French for "blackness"; an attitude formed in the 1920s and 1930s by African intellectuals educated and living in Europe that stressed racial pride, self-confidence, and joy in black creativity and the black spirit. This Westernized elite pushed for equal access to government jobs, modest steps toward self-government, and an end to discrimination in their home countries.

neocolonialism The continuing Western economic domination of supposedly independent countries in Latin America, Asia, and Africa.

Neo-Confucianism The revival of Confucian thinking that began in eleventh-century China. It maintained that a true Confucian would reject Buddhism and reasserted the Confucian commitment to moral perfection and the betterment of society. However, Neo-Confucianist writings often incorporated Buddhist and Daoist elements. *See also* Buddhism, Daoism.

neo-liberalism An approach to the world economy, developed in the 1970s, that favored reduced tariffs, the free movement of capital, a mobile and temporary workforce, the privatization of industry, and the curtailing of government efforts to regulate the economy.

Neolithic era A phase of human history dating from the beginnings of agriculture (about 10,000–12,000 years ago) to the rise of urban-based civilizations. It generated permanently settled communities, growing populations, and technological advances in pottery, weaving, and metallurgy. These developments in turn laid the foundation for the subsequent emergence of cities, states, and civilizations. The Neolithic era gave way to the era of agrarian civilizations much earlier in some areas (Egypt, Mesopotamia, Indus River Valley, China, coastal Peru) than in others. In parts of sub-Saharan Africa, Central Asia, the Americas, and elsewhere, a Neolithic style of life endured into modern times. *See also* Agricultural Revolution.

neo-Malthusian A belief of social scientists, based on the late-eighteenth-century works of Thomas Malthus (1766–1834), that population tends to grow faster than the food supply. The fear of famine prompted some governments in Africa, Asia, and Latin America to push family planning in the 1950s and 1960s, although cultural and religious opposition to birth control meant birthrates were slow to fall.

NEP *See* New Economic Policy.

Nestorianism The Christian doctrine that maintained that Jesus had two distinct and separate natures—one human and the other divine. This doctrine was originally promulgated by Nestorius, named bishop of Constantinople in 428 C.E. Condemned by the orthodox hierarchy, his followers, the Nestorians, formed a new church in Persia that flourished until 1300.

New Christians Spanish Jews who converted to Christianity in the fourteenth century to avoid persecution by anti-Semitic pogroms. *See also* pogrom.

New Culture Movement An intellectual revolution founded in China by young Western-oriented intellectuals around 1916. It attacked traditional Chinese, particularly Confucian, culture and promoted Western ideas of science, democracy, and individualism. *See also* May Fourth Movement.

New Deal A series of government reforms and economic interventions enacted between 1933 and 1942 by the Franklin D. Roosevelt (1933–1945) administration in the United States with the goal of ending the Great Depression.

New Economic Policy (NEP) The 1921 policy created by Vladimir Lenin (r. 1917–1924) that reestablished limited economic freedom in the Soviet Union to rebuild agriculture and industry in the face of economic disintegration. In a concession to capitalism, the policy allowed peasants to sell their grain on the market and entrepreneurs to engage in trade and keep the profits.

new imperialism The rush of European countries to claim territories in Africa and Asia in the late nineteenth century. *See also* scramble for Africa.

NGO *See* non-governmental organization.

nirvana The end goal of Buddhism, in which individual identity is "extinguished" into a state of serenity and great compassion with freedom from reincarnation.

nomads Pastoral peoples who depend on their domesticated animals (cattle, sheep, goats, horses, camels) and who move systematically from place to place to provide food, water, and pastures for the animals.

non-governmental organization (NGO) A charitable foundation or activist group such as Doctors Without Borders that often works internationally on political, economic, and relief issues, shaping policies and the course of political reform. The term first came into use with the establishment of the United Nations in 1945, although such organizations have existed since the nineteenth century.

North American Free Trade Agreement (NAFTA) A 1994 treaty that established a free-trade zone between the United States, Mexico, and Canada by providing for the elimination of tariffs and other economic barriers. Its intent was to encourage economic growth and raise the standard of living in these regions.

North Atlantic Treaty Organization (NATO) The military alliance formed in 1949 to provide security for the United States, Canada, and their allies in Western Europe and Scandinavia against potential Soviet aggression. The corresponding alliance of the Soviet Union and its allies was known as the Warsaw Pact.

North/South gap The sharp economic disparity between the rich northern nations and the poorer or developing southern countries of the world that has emerged since Europe's Industrial Revolution in the early nineteenth century. Great controversy exists over whether that gap has been widening or lessening in recent decades.

Nuremberg Laws A series of laws passed by the Nazi-dominated German parliament in 1935 that forbade sexual relations between Jews and other Germans and mandated that Jews identify themselves in public by wearing the Star of David.

O

OAU *See* Organization of African Unity.

oba The title of the king of Benin, a small kingdom along the west African coast.

October Manifesto A document reluctantly issued by the Russian tsar in response to the revolutionary upheavals of 1905. It granted full civil rights to Russian citizens and promised a popularly elected Duma (parliament) with real legislative power. *See also* Duma.

oligarchy A type of government in which a small group of wealthy individuals or families, not necessarily of aristocratic birth, rules.

OPEC *See* Organization of Petroleum Exporting Countries.

Opium Wars Two wars fought between Western powers and China (1839–1842 and 1856–1858) in response to long-standing Chinese restrictions on trade with the West and provoked initially by Chinese efforts to halt the flow of opium into their country. China lost both wars and was forced to make major concessions.

oracle bone In ancient Chinese civilization, an animal bone that was heated and the cracks within it interpreted as prophecies. The prophecies were written on the bone and provide the earliest sources for ancient Chinese writing.

Organization of African Unity (OAU) Founded in 1963, a group of African states that sought to end European colonialism in Africa and promote cooperation and solidarity among newly independent African nations, believing that acting as a collective force would aid their long-term success.

Organization of Petroleum Exporting Countries (OPEC) A consortium of oil-producing countries, consisting primarily of Arab nations of the Middle East, founded in 1960 to regulate the supply and exportation of oil.

outcaste A large category of jatis at the bottom of India's caste system. Most were associated with occupations deemed ritually impure, such as slaughtering animals or sweeping up the filth of the village; they were also known as "Untouchables," for even the touch of such a person rendered others ritually impure. *See also* caste system.

P

pagan From the Latin term meaning "a country-dweller"; within the Christian world, a follower of a non-Christian religion, often a polytheistic or shamanistic tradition. In the time of early Christianity, it referred to a person who worshipped the Greco-Roman gods.

Paleolithic era The long period of human history before the development of agriculture when people used only stone tools. In this era (ca. 200,000–10,000 B.C.E.) people did not usually settle permanently in one place but moved seasonally as they hunted, fished, and gathered wild grains, fruits, and nuts. *See also* Neolithic era.

Palestine Liberation Organization (PLO) A loose union of Palestinian refugee groups created in 1964 that opposed Israel and sought to work toward Palestinian home rule.

Pan-Africanism A twentieth-century political ideology that stressed the common bonds of all people of African descent both on the African continent and beyond. Associated with the struggle against colonial rule, the movement formally began with the first Pan-African Congress convened in London in 1900 and was followed by several similar congresses attended by intellectuals from both Africa and the Americas.

Paris Peace Accord An international agreement in 1973 designed to bring about an end to the United States' involvement in the Vietnam War. It resulted in the withdrawal of the U.S. military, which had had a presence in the country since 1965. The struggle between Communist and non-Communist forces continued, however, and a total Communist victory followed in 1975.

Partition of India The division of the British Indian Empire into two independent states in 1947: India, which was mostly Hindu, and Pakistan, which was mostly Muslim. Millions of people had to move between countries, and well over 500,000 people died in the ensuing confusion.

pastoralism A way of life in which people depended on the herding of domesticated animals for their food. Pastoral nomads led their animals to seasonal grazing grounds rather than settling permanently in a single location. This food-producing strategy could be adapted to regions unsuited for agriculture.

paterfamilias The oldest dominant male of the family, one who holds nearly absolute power over the lives of his family during his lifetime. In ancient Rome, sons could not legally own property until the death of their father.

patriarchy A gender system in which men hold dominant authority within the family and society.

patrician A member of the aristocracy in the Roman Republic. Until the third century B.C.E., only these wealthy landowners could hold political or religious offices. *See also* plebeian.

patrilineal society A society in which people trace ancestry and descent through the male side of the family and property is typically passed from father to son. *See also* matrilineal society.

patronage A social arrangement in which wealthy and elite individuals, or patrons, offer support to socially inferior clients in exchange for the client's loyalty and obedience. The term also refers to the practice of elite groups in endowing religious, charitable, or artistic endeavors.

pax Mongolica The environment of political and economic stability within the Mongol Empire during the thirteenth and fourteenth centuries that facilitated trade and travel throughout Eurasia.

pax Romana The period of relative stability and peace in the Roman Empire in the first and second centuries. The rule of the first Roman emperor, Augustus (r. 27 B.C.E.–14 C.E.), ushered in 200 years of serenity and prosperity, marred only by brief interludes of fighting between generals striving to rule the empire.

Peace of Utrecht A series of treaties written between 1713 and 1715 that ended the War of the Spanish Succession (1701–1714), stopped French expansion in Europe, and marked the rise of the British Empire.

Peace of Westphalia A series of treaties that ended the Thirty Years' War (1618–1648). The treaties represented a great shift in European power, with the Spanish and Austrian Habsburgs both losing several territories and France emerging as the main continental power. *See also* Thirty Years' War.

Peloponnesian War A great war between Athens (and allies) and Sparta (and allies), lasting from 431 to 404 B.C.E. The conflict ended in the defeat of Athens and the closing of Athens's Golden Age.

peninsulares The colonial officials and other natives of Spain and Portugal who lived in the Latin American colonies. Peninsulares controlled trade, and they claimed superiority over the Creoles who had been born in the Americas. *See also* Creoles.

perestroika Russian for "restructuring"; a bold economic program launched in the Soviet Union by Mikhail Gorbachev (r. 1985–1991). Beginning in 1987, the program permitted an easing of government price controls on some goods, more independence for state enterprises, and the setting up of profit-seeking private cooperatives to provide personal services for consumers. *See also* glasnost.

Persian Wars *See* Greco-Persian Wars.

pharaoh The leader of religious and political life in ancient Egypt. Egyptians saw their pharaoh as having divine qualities.

philosophes Eighteenth-century intellectuals of the Enlightenment who wrote on subjects ranging from current affairs to art criticism with the goal of furthering reform in society.

piece of eight A standard Spanish coin, first minted in 1497, that became a medium of exchange in North America, Europe, India, Russia, and West Africa as well as in the Spanish Empire. The coin was worth 8 reales.

Pillars of Islam *See* Five Pillars of Islam.

plantation A large tract of land that produced staple crops for the market such as sugar, coffee, and tobacco, typically with the use of slave labor. The plantation system was used in the Roman Empire and in the American colonies of European powers.

plebeian The common class of citizens in the Roman Republic after 509 B.C.E., essentially those not included in the aristocracy or patrician class. Plebeians struggled for centuries for the right to hold public office. *See also* patrician.

PLO *See* Palestine Liberation Organization.

pochteca Professional merchants in the Aztec Empire (1345–1521) whose wealth often elevated them to elite status.

pogrom Organized violence against a specific ethnic or religious group, particularly Jews. Christian pogroms swept parts of Europe during the Crusades (1096–1291) and after the Black Death (1347–1351) as they sought a scapegoat for the disease;

Russian Jews experienced a series of pogroms during the late nineteenth and early twentieth centuries.

polis An independent city-state based on citizenship that developed in Greece in the eighth century B.C.E. Unlike earlier city-states ruled by a monarchy, the Greek polis was a community of citizens, not subjects, who often governed themselves under varying political systems.

polytheism The worship of multiple gods. The majority of early civilizations, including the Egyptians, Mesopotamians, and Greeks, were polytheistic and worshipped a variety of gods thought to have power over different areas of human existence, such as war, fertility, and weather. *See also* monotheism.

portolan chart A fifteenth-century description of a maritime route written by Portuguese navigators and showing bays, coves, capes, ports, and the distance between these places.

positivism A theory that holds that the diligent study of facts generates accurate, or "positive," laws of society and these laws could help, in turn, in the formulation of policy and legislation. Developed in the mid-nineteenth century, positivism is based on the work of the French social philosopher Auguste Comte (1798–1857) and forms the foundation of the social sciences.

postmodernism A term applied in the late twentieth century to both an intense mixture of styles in the arts without a central unifying theme and an intellectual critique of Enlightenment and scientific beliefs in rationality and the possibility for precise knowledge.

Prague Spring A sweeping series of liberal reforms instituted by Communist leader Alexander Dubcek in Czechoslovakia in 1968. The movement was subsequently crushed by a Soviet invasion. *See also* Brezhnev Doctrine.

predestination A religious doctrine that held that God, before he created the world, had selected every person for either salvation or damnation. Those who were predestined to be saved, the "elect," were known only to God. Predestination was an important feature in the theology of John Calvin. *See also* Calvinism.

primogeniture The process of inheritance by which the first-born son is the chief beneficiary. Within Europe after the year 1000, primogeniture kept a family's possessions, titles, and authority under one person's control. It also left younger sons without an inheritance or a prospect of marriage; consequently, many lived at the courts of great rulers or joined the church as clerics or monks.

principate A form of government established by Augustus Caesar (r. 27 B.C.E.–14 C.E.), which was headed by a princeps, or "First Citizen," meant to be appointed by the senate. Founded in 27 B.C.E. to quell the violence of the previous century, the princeps in reality served as an emperor and appointed his own heir.

proletariat The urban working class or, in Marxist terms, those who do not own the means of production such as factories, tools, workshops, and machines. The term was originally used in ancient Rome to describe the poorest part of the urban population. *See also* Marxism.

protected people *See* dhimmi.

Protestant Reformation A sixteenth- and seventeenth-century reform movement initiated by Martin Luther (1483–1546) that rejected the rituals, hierarchy, and corruption of the Roman Catholic Church, as well as the authority of the pope, and emphasized individual salvation by faith alone. As it spread throughout Europe, the Reformation took on social, political, and economic dimensions as well, and it gave the middle and peasant classes an opportunity to contest the existing social order.

Protestantism A branch of Christianity that formed when Martin Luther (1483–1546) and his followers separated from the Catholic Church in 1517. Protestantism then broke into a variety of sects, including Quakers, Calvinists, Anglicans, and Anabaptists. Protestantism encouraged individual interpretation of the Bible, without reliance on popes or bishops, and prayer directed to God instead of through Mary, saints, or elaborate rituals.

public sphere An idealized intellectual environment that emerged in Europe in the years following the eighteenth-century Enlightenment, where members of society came together as individuals to discuss issues relevant to the society, economics, and politics of the day. More generally, it refers to life outside the home or the domestic sphere. *See also* separate spheres.

pueblo A communal village built by the peoples of southwestern North America, sometimes consisting of adjoining flat-roofed stone or adobe buildings arranged in terraces.

Punic Wars Three major wars between Rome and Carthage in North Africa, fought between 264 and 146 B.C.E., that culminated in Roman victory and control of the western Mediterranean.

Puranas Hindu religious writings, derived from oral tradition and written down during the first millennium C.E., that included the legends of the gods and great warrior clans.

purdah The Muslim or Hindu practice of veiling women or secluding them in a harem, meant to prevent them from being seen by men not related to them. *See also* harem.

Pure Land Buddhism A school of Mahayana Buddhism originating in China that emphasized the sinfulness of the human condition and the necessity of believing in savior figures (buddhas and bodhisattvas) to gain rebirth in paradise. *See also* bodhisattva.

Purges *See* Great Purges.

Puritanism Strict Calvinists who opposed all vestiges of Catholic ritual in the Church of England. The Puritans became influential in the late sixteenth century during the reign of Elizabeth I and undercut the authority of crown-appointed bishops by taking control of church administration themselves. The issue remained a source of tension in the seventeenth century and was a main factor leading to the English Civil War (1642–1646).

putsch *See* coup d'état.

putting-out system A method of manufacturing that was widely used for textile production in pre-industrial societies. Raw materials were distributed to families who turned them into finished products at home. The putting-out system provided peasant families with a supplemental income and allowed manufacturers to escape the restrictions of the urban guilds.

pyramid The burial place of an Egyptian pharaoh, mostly built during the Old Kingdom (2663–2195 B.C.E.) and containing all things needed for the afterlife. It also symbolized the king's power and his connection with the sun god.

Q

qadis Muslim judges who carried out the judicial functions of the state.

qi In Chinese belief, the vital energy of the cosmos. The concept of qi and li (principle) were developed by Confucian teachers during the eleventh century in response to the sophisticated metaphysics of Buddhism.

quadrivium *See* trivium.

Quechua The official language of the Incas in the fifteenth century. Conquered peoples were forced to adopt the language, and it is still spoken by most Peruvians.

quinto The one-fifth of all precious metals mined in the Americas that the Spanish monarchy claimed as its own, beginning in 1504. Gold and silver from the colonies made up 25 percent of the Crown's income.

quipu *See* khipu.

Quran The book recording the revelations of the prophet Muhammad (ca. 570–632 C.E.) that is regarded as the most sacred scripture in Islam.

R

raja From an ancient Indo-European word meaning "to rule"; an Indian monarch, princely ruler, or chieftain who led his people into battle and governed them during peacetime.

Rape of Nanjing The Japanese invasion of Nanjing, China, in 1937–1938 that resulted in the rape, torture, and murder of vast numbers of civilians.

rationalism The general opinion among eighteenth-century Enlightenment thinkers that nothing should be accepted on faith and that everything should be subjected to secular, critical examination. More generally, rationalism is an approach to knowledge based on human inquiry rather than divine revelation.

realpolitik Policies associated initially with nation building that are said to be based on hard-headed realities rather than the romantic notions or ideals of earlier nationalists. Its goals center on strengthening the state and tightening social order. Originally coined by European leaders following the failed revolutions of 1848, the term has come to mean any policy based on considerations of power alone.

reconquista Christian wars of conquest against the Muslim kingdoms of medieval Spain. Leaders of the reconquista cast Muslims as outsiders, even though they had been integrated into Spanish society, and believed it was their sacred and patriotic mission to expel Muslims from the country.

Red Guards Young militant supporters of the Communist Party and Chairman Mao Zedong (r. 1949–1976) during the Cultural Revolution of 1966–1969. Seeking to rid China of anyone they identified as an enemy, they attacked government officials, teachers, intellectuals, and factory managers around the country. *See also* Cultural Revolution.

Reichstag The popularly elected lower house of government of the new German Empire after 1871. Originally established in the fifteenth century to control feuding among the princes and with the emperor, the Reichstag was a national assembly of princes, electors, and representatives from the cities.

Reign of Terror The period from 1793 to 1794, during which revolutionary leader Maximilien Robespierre (1758–1794) used violence to solidify the home front of France under its new government. Some 40,000 French men and women were executed or died in prison.

reincarnation The Indian belief system that every living being's soul can be reborn in another body after death in a long cycle of existence. Both Hinduism and Buddhism hold that it is possible to escape the cycle and achieve the exalted state of nirvana (Buddhism) or moksha (Hinduism).

relic A material object associated with the life of a saint, such as a bone or scrap of clothing, used to invoke the blessing and protection of that particular saint.

Renaissance French for "rebirth"; a period of revival and flourishing in learning and the arts. The term most commonly refers to the intellectual and artistic movement that began in Italy in the fifteenth century and influenced the rest of Europe in the sixteenth; it was characterized by a renewed interest in the classical teachings of Greece and Rome and their application to politics, society, and culture. *See also* Carolingian Renaissance.

reparations Payment, usually in the form of money or goods, made by the losing party in a conflict with the intention of compensating the winning party for damage incurred during the war. Reparations may also be made in the case of a human rights violation, such as forced labor or imprisonment. *See also* Dawes Plan, war guilt clause.

repartimiento The system developed during the sixteenth century in which natives of the Latin American colonies under Spanish control were forced to labor on colonial plantations or in mines owned by the Crown. Although the natives were technically free and the work was only for a limited amount of time, they were often treated like slaves.

representative government A political system in which people elect officials to represent them and serve as their voice in the government. *See also* constitutionalism.

republic A political system characterized by the absence of a monarch and by the active participation of at least some of the people in the affairs of state.

revisionism An effort by moderate German socialists at the end of the nineteenth century to update Marxian doctrines to reflect the realities of the time. Revisionists claimed that Karl Marx's predictions of ever-greater poverty for workers had proven false; therefore, instead of advocating a violent uprising, they should work more gradually toward rights for the working class.

Revolutionary Right Also known as Radical Nationalism, a movement in Japanese political life (ca. 1930–1945) that was marked by extreme nationalism, a commitment to elite leadership focused around the emperor, and dedication to foreign expansion.

romanticism A European philosophical and artistic movement of the late eighteenth and early nineteenth centuries that glorified nature, emotion, genius, and the imagination. Romanticism emerged partly in reaction to the Enlightenment's excessive reliance on reason.

Royal African Company A trading company chartered in 1660 to bring slaves from West Africa to English colonies in the Americas. It held a monopoly over the English slave trade until about 1700.

Russian Revolution of 1905 A rebellion that erupted in Russia after the country's defeat at the hands of Japan, during a time in which people were already deeply dissatisfied with the tsar. The revolution was suppressed, but it forced the government to make substantial reforms. *See also* Bloody Sunday, Russo-Japanese War.

Russian Revolution of 1917 A massive revolutionary upheaval that overthrew the Romanov dynasty (1613–1917) in Russia and ended with the seizure of power by Communists under the leadership of Vladimir Lenin (r. 1917–1924). *See also* Bolshevik.

Russo-Japanese War The 1904–1905 war between Russia and Japan, fought over imperial influence and territory in China, particularly in Manchuria. Japan's victory established the country as a formidable military competitor in East Asia and precipitated the Russian Revolution of 1905. *See also* Russian Revolution of 1905.

S

sacrament A religious ritual performed by Christians and believed to be a vehicle for divine grace. For Roman Catholics, sacraments include baptism, holy communion, ordination, confession, and marriage. The validity of the sacraments—how and by whom they should be performed—was a frequent source of religious conflict in medieval and early modern Europe.

saint An individual who had lived a particularly holy life and was consequently accorded great honor by medieval Christians. Saints were believed to possess the power to work miracles and were frequently invoked for healing and protection.

salon An informal gathering, usually sponsored by a middle-class or aristocratic woman, that provided a forum for new ideas and an opportunity to establish new intellectual contacts among supporters of the Enlightenment in the eighteenth century.

samsara In Hinduism, the transmigration of souls by a continual process of rebirth.

samurai The warrior class that dominated Japanese society and culture from the twelfth to the nineteenth centuries. The samurai, guided by the value system *bushido*, evolved from being armed retainers of feudal lords to an administrative elite. *See also* bushido.

sati A practice in which a high-caste Hindu woman threw herself on her husband's funeral pyre. The belief was that by doing so, both her and her husband's sins would be forgiven and they could enjoy eternal bliss in Heaven.

satrapy A province of the ancient Persian Empire administered by a regional, semi-independent governor, or satrap. The office of the satrap was originally an Assyrian government institution, but it was successfully adopted by the Persian king Cyrus (r. ca. 559–530 B.C.E.). In the decentralized yet effective Persian system, the satrap's duties included maintaining order, enlisting troops as needed, and sending revenues to the royal treasury.

satyagraha The political philosophy of Mohandas Gandhi (1869–1948), which advocated confrontational but nonviolent political action, striving for truth and social justice through love, suffering, and conversion of the oppressor.

savanna Flat grasslands with scattered trees and scrubs that account for perhaps 55 percent of the African continent. Wetter savanna regions encouraged early African peoples to develop grain-based agriculture.

schism *See* Great Schism.

scholar-gentry class China's long-standing elite or ruling class, which derived their status from both land-holding and office-holding. The scholar-gentry class developed during the Han dynasty (206 B.C.E.–220 C.E.), which gave a privileged position to men trained in the Confucian classics.

Scholasticism A method of thinking, reasoning, and writing, developed by medieval professors, in which questions were raised and authorities cited on both sides of the question.

Scientific Revolution An intellectual and cultural movement between the mid-sixteenth and early eighteenth centuries that stressed the use of careful observations, controlled experiments, and mathematically defined laws to determine how the world worked. These new methods and theories often clashed with biblical teachings or the long-accepted explanations of classical philosophers; they came under fire from other scientists and church authorities but formed the basis for modern science.

scramble for Africa The late-nineteenth-century process by which European imperial powers carved up the African continent into colonial territories. Although European powers managed this process without war among themselves, it was a bloody process of conquest in many parts of the continent. *See also* Berlin Conference.

scurvy A disease resulting from a deficiency of vitamin C and common to sailors who had no access to fresh fruit and vegetables on extended sea voyages. It caused wounds to reopen, bleeding gums, and diarrhea, and was ultimately fatal if left untreated.

SEATO *See* Southeast Asia Treaty Organization.

secularization The shift from a traditional, religion-based way of thinking to a modern, rational, scientific approach to understanding the world.

Security Council The United Nations body created in 1945 that has the authority to examine international conflicts, impose economic and political penalties on an aggressor, and even use force, if necessary, to restore international peace and security. It consists of five permanent member-nations (China, Russia, France, the United Kingdom, and the United States) and ten rotating members.

self-strengthening movement China's limited program of internal reform in the 1860s and 1870s that aimed to reinvigorate traditional techniques of Chinese governance, modernize the military along Western lines, and bring Chinese industry closer to par with the industrial progress of the West.

semi-sedentary A term used to describe the peoples of the eastern woodlands of the United States, Central America, the Amazon basin, and the Caribbean islands who combined partial reliance on agriculture with gathering and hunting.

senate Originating under the Etruscans and adopted by the Romans, a council of noble elders who deliberated important issues of state and advised the king in the Roman Empire.

separate spheres A rigid gender division of labor, prompted by industrialization in the nineteenth century, with the wife as mother and homemaker and the husband as wage earner. Improving economic conditions meant that only poor wives had to work outside the home, and better-off women were discouraged from doing so.

separatism Radical demands for ethnic autonomy or political independence. Competition among ethnic groups in Africa and Eurasia has fostered separatism and a number of violent civil wars in the late twentieth and early twenty-first centuries.

sepoy A member of India's native troops who were trained as infantrymen under British colonial rule.

Sepoy Mutiny *See* Indian Rebellion.

serf A peasant legally bound to the land he or she worked and owing goods, labor, and service to the lord who owned the land. In Latin Christendom serfdom gradually eroded in the centuries after 1400, but in Russia serfs were not emancipated until 1861.

service nobility Russian troops upon whom a nonhereditary noble title was bestowed as a result of their military service to Ivan IV (r. 1530–1584) in the sixteenth century.

settler colony A territory in which the colonizing people settled in large numbers, rather than simply sending relatively small numbers to govern and exploit the region.

Seven Years' War   A conflict (1756–1763) between England and France and their allies that was fought in Europe, the Americas, and Asia. Upon its loss, France was forced to relinquish its territories in India and Canada to the British and the Louisiana Territory to the Spanish.

shaman   A person believed to have the ability to act as a bridge between living humans and supernatural forces, often by means of trances induced by psychoactive drugs.

shantytown   An area of makeshift squatter settlements created by a group of the urban poor in Third World cities.

sharia   The whole body of Islamic law, drawn from the Quran, the hadith, and traditions of legal interpretation, that governs the social, political, commercial, and religious lives of Muslims.

sharif   The chief magistrate of Mecca, the holiest city in the Muslim world.

shaykh   A Sufi teacher who attracted a circle of disciples. Shaykhs often founded individual schools of Sufism. *See also* Sufism.

shi   The lower ranks of Chinese aristocracy, who could serve in either military or civil capacities.

Shia   One of the two main branches of Islam, which maintains that only descendants of Muhammad (ca. 570–632 C.E.) through his cousin and son-in-law Ali (r. 656–661 C.E.) have a legitimate right to serve as caliph. Shias believe that their leaders, the imams, have a religious authority that the caliphs lack and that only the imams can reveal the true meaning of the Quran and the wishes of Allah. *See also* Sunni.

Shinto   An ancient Japanese religious tradition focused on kami, or spirits of ancestors and nature. It was elevated to an official state cult in the late nineteenth century.

shogun   A supreme military commander in Japan who also took political control. The title was first taken by Minamoto Yoritomo in 1185, who effectively ruled Japan in the name of the emperor.

show trials   Public false confessions by prominent Communists to plots against Joseph Stalin (r. 1929–1953), elicited by means of threats and torture. Show trials were a key component of Stalin's Great Purges, enacted in the Soviet Union in 1936–1937. *See also* Great Purges.

Sikhism A religion that evolved in India and blended elements of Islam and Hinduism, founded by Guru Nanak (1469–1539), a former follower of the bhakti movement. His teachings rejected caste distinctions and the inequality of men and women.

Silk Roads The various branches of a 4,000-mile-long caravan route that connected China in the east to the Mediterranean Sea in the west, passing through regions such as India and the Middle East. It acquired its name when the Roman Empire used it to import silk from China in exchange for wool, gold, and silver.

Sino-Japanese War An 1894–1895 war between Japan and China, fought over Japanese efforts to separate Korea from Chinese influence and ending in a Japanese victory.

skepticism A philosophy that holds that total certainty about anything is never possible. Originating in ancient Greece, it was revived in the sixteenth century as religious violence and global exploration shook the confidence Westerners had in traditional knowledge. By questioning customary authority, skeptical thought opened the way for new ways of thinking about science, religion, and politics.

slash-and-burn agriculture A system in which farmers cut down part of the forest and burn the vegetation in order to clear patches for cultivation.

Slavophilia A form of Russian nationalism in the mid-nineteenth century that opposed efforts to follow Western models of industrial development and constitutional government. Rejecting rationality and individualism, Slavophiles instead sought to maintain rural traditions and the centrality of the Russian Orthodox Church.

smallpox A highly contagious disease characterized by a rash of blisters and a high fever. Japan's contact with the Chinese mainland led to a smallpox epidemic in 735–737, which is thought to have reduced the Japanese population by 30 percent. Deadly enough in Europe, smallpox later devastated native populations of European colonies, who had no natural immunity to the disease.

social contract The doctrine that all political authority derives not from divine right but from an implicit contract between citizens and their rulers. The idea emerged from the writings of English philosophers Thomas Hobbes (1588–1679) and John Locke (1632–1704) in the second half of the seventeenth century, although each came to different conclusions. Hobbes argued that the social contract gave a ruler absolute power, while Locke claimed it implied a constitutional agreement between the ruler and representatives of his or her subjects.

Social Darwinism A belief that took its inspiration from Charles Darwin's idea of natural selection, arguing that in the economic and political realms, only the fittest would survive. Social Darwinists in the late nineteenth and early twentieth centuries used a distorted version of evolutionary theory to lobby for racist, sexist, and nationalist policies, including the continuation of European imperialism and the advancement of eugenics, or controlled breeding that sought to eliminate the "undesirable" characteristics of the human race. *See also* evolution.

socialism A social and political ideology that emerged in the early nineteenth century in response to the upheaval brought about by industrialization. Taking liberalism a step further, socialists advocated a complete reorganization of society and the need to restore social harmony through communities based on cooperation rather than competition. Many socialists were utopians who believed that the elimination of private property would end social tensions and inspire mutual cooperation. *See also* communism, liberalism, Marxism, utopian socialism.

Socratic Method The type of instruction favored by Socrates (469–399 B.C.E.), the most famous philosopher of Athens' Golden Age. Socrates did not teach through direct instruction but used a conversational approach in which he asked probing questions to make his listeners examine their most cherished assumptions before arriving at their own conclusions.

Solidarity An organization of Polish workers, founded in 1980 and led by Lech Walesa (b. 1943), that became a free and democratic trade union. It contested Communist Party programs and eventually succeeded in ousting the party from the Polish government.

Son of Heaven *See* Mandate of Heaven.

Sophist A new kind of Greek teacher who first appeared around 450 B.C.E. Popular among men with political aspirations, Sophists were controversial because they challenged traditional beliefs by teaching new skills of persuasion in speaking and new ways of thinking about philosophy and religion.

South African War *See* Boer War.

Southeast Asia Treaty Organization (SEATO) The cold war alliance of Western powers and pro-Western countries close to or part of Southeast Asia, formed in 1954 to prevent the spread of communism in the area. Meant to be a counterpart to NATO (North Atlantic Treaty Organization), dissent among the group's members from the beginning made it ineffective, and SEATO dissolved in 1977.

sovereignty The exercise of complete and autonomous control over a political body that is a fundamental goal of all states.

soviet A representative council of workers and soldiers, first formed in Russia during the Revolution of 1905. Soviets played a major role in the Revolution of 1917, and the Bolsheviks used them as the core of their new government.

Spanish-American War A conflict between the United States and Spain, fought in 1898, in which the United States claimed the Philippines. The Filipinos fought alongside the Americans, hoping to gain their freedom; instead, they simply found themselves under a new colonial power.

spinning jenny A machine, invented by James Hargreaves in 1765, that enabled workers to spin cotton at a much faster rate than using a spinning wheel. The subsequent growth of cotton mills in England launched the Industrial Revolution.

stagflation The unusual combination of a stagnant economy and soaring inflation that emerged in the West in the 1970s as a result of an OPEC embargo on oil. *See also* Organization of Petroleum Exporting Countries.

Stalinism A style of government named after the regime of Joseph Stalin (r. 1929–1953), who claimed to operate the Soviet Union under Marxist principles but ruled as a dictator and demanded total allegiance from the people between 1929 and 1953. He created an atmosphere of terror to suppress political dissent. *See also* Great Purges, show trials.

state A political system that exercises sole sovereign authority over a defined territory and its inhabitants through institutions such as armed forces, a civil service or bureaucracy, courts, and police.

stateless society A village-based agricultural community that operated through kinship principles and functioned without a formal government apparatus.

steam engine A mechanical device in which the steam from heated water builds up pressure to drive a piston or work a pump, rather than relying on human or animal muscle power. Although primitive versions were developed earlier, the introduction of a more sophisticated engine in the late eighteenth century allowed a hitherto unimagined increase in productivity and made the Industrial Revolution possible.

steppe The arid grasslands of Central Asia. While too dry for agriculture, the steppe could support grazing animals and so were home to many nomadic herding societies.

stoicism A philosophy that considers nature an expression of divine will and holds that people can be happy only when living in accordance with nature. Stoicism became a popular philosophy in ancient Greece and one that later captured the minds of many Romans.

stupa A Buddhist monument, usually bell- or dome-shaped, that holds a part of the Buddha's remains or an object connected to him. There are numerous stupas throughout India and other parts of Asia.

Sudra The lowest of the major Indian caste groupings, or varnas. Its members were regarded as servants of their social betters. The Sudra varna eventually included peasant farmers. *See also* caste system.

Sufis Islamic mystics, many of whom were important missionaries of Islam in conquered lands and who were revered as saints.

Sufism A tradition within Islam that emphasized mystical knowledge and personal experience of the divine over obedience to the dictates of Islamic law and scripture. It became widely popular by the ninth and tenth centuries.

sultan An Arabic word originally used by the Seljuk Turks to mean a leader with authority or dominion; later adopted by the Ottomans to connote a supreme political and military leader.

Sunna From the Arabic for "trodden path"; the deeds and sayings of Muhammad (ca. 570–632 C.E.), which constitute the obligatory example for Muslim life.

Sunni One of the two main branches of Islam, which adheres to the practices and beliefs of Muhammad (ca. 570–632 C.E.) described in the Sunna. Sunnis accept the historical succession of caliphs as legitimate leaders of the Muslim community and believe that religious authority emerges from the larger community, especially from the religious scholars known as ulama. *See also* Shia, ulama.

sutras The written teachings of the Buddha, first transcribed in the second or first century B.C.E. Until that point, the Buddha's followers had transmitted his teachings orally.

Sykes-Picot Agreement The 1916 secret agreement between Britain and France that divided up the Arab lands of Lebanon, Syria, southern Turkey, Palestine, Jordan, and Iraq, despite British promises of Arab independence after World War I (1914–1918).

syncretism The merging or blending of different religious, philosophical, or cultural traditions. Sikhism, a blend of Islam and Hinduism, is one example of a syncretic faith.

T

Taika reforms Efforts made by the Japanese prince Shotoku (574–622) to strengthen Japan with Chinese ideas. He borrowed concepts about centralized government, land reform, and architecture and developed the "Seventeen Principles" in 604, which drew from both Confucian and Buddhist teachings.

Taiping Rebellion An internal rebellion in China that devastated much of the country between 1850 and 1864 and resulted in some 20 million deaths. Its leader, Hong Xiuquan, claimed he was the younger brother of Jesus and rejected Confucianism, Buddhism, and Daoism in favor of a unique form of Christianity. Hong and his followers demanded revolutionary change and sought to overthrow the Qing dynasty (1644–1911), but were stopped by the armies of landowners who feared the radical program.

Taliban An Islamic fundamentalist organization that controlled Afghanistan from 1996 to 2002. Since falling from power, the Taliban have been funding and protecting poor Afghan opium poppy farmers in exchange for new recruits and profits from the opium trade.

Talmud A religious work composed between 70 and 636 C.E. that records civil and ceremonial law and Jewish legend.

Tanzimat reforms Turkish for "reorganization"; radical reforms to the Ottoman Empire that were designed to remake the empire on a Western European model, beginning in 1839. The sultan called for new factories, technologies, schools, and courts and proclaimed equality for all citizens, regardless of their religion.

tariff A government's way of supporting and aiding its own economy by laying high taxes on the cheaper goods imported from another country.

tax-farming A system for tax collection that involved contracting that function to private parties in exchange for a share of the taxes they collected. Practiced in many parts of the world, it was rife with possibilities for corruption and abuse.

Terror (France) The term used to describe the revolutionary violence in France in 1793–1794, when radicals under the leadership of Maximilien Robespierre (1758–1794) executed tens of thousands of people deemed enemies of the revolution.

Terror (Soviet Union) *See* Great Purges.

terrorism Coordinated and targeted political violence by opposition groups, often designed to have both military and psychological consequences on its victims.

theme A military district of the Byzantine Empire (330–1453) that was governed by a general who held both civil and military authority.

theocracy A government in which the leader rules in the name of a god.

Theravada Buddhism Sanskrit for "the teaching of the elders"; the early form of Buddhism according to which the Buddha was a wise teacher but not divine. Theravada Buddhism emphasized practices rather than beliefs. Gods did not play much of a role in helping people toward Enlightenment and instead left them to find it on their own.

Thermidorian reaction The period in France after the execution of Maximilien Robespierre (1758–1794), which was a reaction to the despotism of the Reign of Terror. *See also* Terror (France).

Third Estate In prerevolutionary France, the term used for the 98 percent of the population that was neither clerical nor noble, and for their representatives at the Estates General. In 1789, the Third Estate declared itself a National Assembly and launched the French Revolution (1789–1799).

Third Rome The term used for Moscow in the fifteenth century, as some Russian church leaders claimed to be the successors to the Byzantine Empire (330–1453). The Byzantine capital, Constantinople, was referred to as the "second Rome."

Third World A term devised after World War II (1939–1945) to designate those countries outside either the capitalist world of the U.S. bloc or the socialist world of the Soviet bloc, many of which were emerging from imperial domination. The term came to refer to countries that were less industrialized than the Western or Soviet regions.

Thirty Years' War A violent struggle between Catholics and Protestants that began in the Holy Roman Empire in 1618 and eventually involved most of Europe. By the time peace was achieved in 1648, an estimated one-third of urban residents and two-thirds of the rural population had been killed, and trade and agriculture were upended.

Three Emperors' League A conservative alliance formed in 1873 that linked the monarchs of Austria-Hungary, Germany, and Russia against radical movements.

three-field system An agricultural innovation that gained popularity in eighth-century Europe in which one field was planted with spring crops, one with autumn crops, and one was left fallow, or unplanted. The rotation made for richer soil and a more varied diet.

three obediences In Chinese Confucian thought, the notion that a woman is permanently subordinate to male control: first to that of her father, then of her husband, and finally of her son.

Tiananmen Square demonstration A protest led by pro-democracy Chinese students in 1989 at which Communists imposed martial law and arrested, injured, or killed hundreds of students.

timar A land grant given in compensation for military service by the Ottoman sultan to a soldier. The practice was maintained from the fourteenth to the sixteenth centuries and was the only form of pay the soldier received.

TNC *See* transnational corporation.

Torah The first five books of the Hebrew Bible, also known as the Pentateuch. The Torah, written about 950 B.C.E., provided many of the laws and traditions for the Jewish people to follow.

total war A war built on the full mobilization of soldiers, civilians, and the technological capacities of the nations involved. Governments encourage national unity through propaganda and take control of social and economic life to make the greatest possible military effort. The World Wars of the twentieth century are often characterized as total wars.

totalitarianism A single-party form of government emerging after World War I (1914–1918) in which the ruling political party seeks to penetrate and control all parts of the social, cultural, economic, and political lives of the population. A totalitarian state typically makes use of mass communication and violence to instill its ideology and maintain power. Nazi Germany and the Soviet Union under Joseph Stalin (r. 1929–1953) are commonly cited examples.

trade diaspora   A network of merchants from the same city or region who live permanently in foreign lands and cooperate with each other to pursue trading opportunities.

trading post empire   A form of imperial dominance based on control of trade rather than on control of subject peoples or territory. In the sixteenth century, the Portuguese created a trading post empire in the Indian Ocean as they sought to dominate the spice trade.

trance dance   A nightlong ritual, practiced in the San culture of Southern Africa, to activate a human being's inner spiritual potency (n/um) to counteract the evil influences of gods and ancestors. The practice was apparently common to the Khoisan people, of whom the Ju/'hoansi are a surviving remnant.

transnational corporation (TNC)   A huge global business that produces goods or delivers services simultaneously in many countries. TNCs have helped to speed along economic globalization.

trans-Saharan slave trade   A fairly small-scale but long-lived trade that developed in the twelfth century, exporting West African slaves captured in raids across the Sahara for sale mostly as household servants in Islamic North Africa. The difficulty of travel across the desert limited the scope of this trade.

transubstantiation   The belief advanced by the Catholic Church that when bread and wine are consecrated by the priest at Mass, they are transformed into the actual body and blood of Christ. *See also* Eucharist.

Treaty of Guadalupe Hidalgo   The 1848 treaty with the United States in which Mexico surrendered its claims to Texas, yielded New Mexico and California, and recognized the Rio Grande as the international border.

Treaty of Lausanne   The 1923 treaty that ended the Turkish war against Greece and their British allies and recognized the territorial integrity of a truly independent Turkey.

Treaty of Nanjing   The 1842 treaty that ended the first Opium War (1839–1842). It opened five ports to international trade, fixed the tariff on imported goods, imposed an indemnity on China to cover Britain's war expenses, and ceded the island of Hong Kong to Britain. *See also* Opium Wars.

Treaty of Verdun   The 843 treaty that divided the territories of Charlemagne (r. 768–814) between his three surviving grandsons and formed the precursor states of present-day Germany, France, and Italy.

Treaty of Versailles   The central component of the Peace of Paris (1919–1920), which effectively ended World War I (1914–1918). The immense penalties it placed on Germany are regarded as one of the causes of World War II (1939–1945).

trench warfare   A combat style in which soldiers dug deep trenches along either side of a contested area. Trench warfare became widely prevalent during World War I (1914–1918), especially on the Western Front, in response to the new offensive firepower of machine guns and mustard gas. The cost in lives was staggering and the gains in territory minimal.

tribune   A political office created around 450 B.C.E. to provide plebeians a voice in Roman government. Tribunes were a special panel of ten annually elected officials whose only duty was to stop actions that would harm plebeians or their property. The establishment of this office paved the way for plebeians to ultimately serve in all ranks of the government.

tribute   The payment of money, gifts, or even people to a ruling authority. Tributes could be made by a feudal vassal to his lord or by rulers or nations, to acknowledge their submission to another ruler or to cover the cost of protection.

Triple Alliance (1428)   The agreement between the Mexica and two other nearby city-states that launched the Aztec Empire (1345–1521).

Triple Alliance (1882)   A treaty between Austria, Germany, and Italy that called for joint response if any one of the signatories were attacked. It was fundamental to the diplomatic structure of World War I (1914–1918).

Triple Entente   The alliance of Great Britain, France, and Russia in World War I (1914–1918).

trivium   The first three of the seven liberal arts, namely grammar, rhetoric, and logic, regarded as the foundation of education in medieval European universities. The rest of the liberal arts consist of mathematical sciences—the quadrivium of arithmetic, geometry, music, and astronomy.

troubadour A medieval poet in southern Europe who wrote and sang lyrical verses devoted to the themes of love, desire, beauty, and gallantry.

tsar Slavic for "caesar"; the Russian imperial title first taken by Muscovite prince Ivan III (r. 1462–1505). The last Russian tsar, Nicholas II (r. 1894–1917), was forced to abdicate in 1917 as a result of the Russian Revolution.

Twelver Shiism A branch of Shia Islam whose followers believed that twelve leaders or *imams* ordained by Allah inherited the spiritual and political power held by Muhammad (ca. 570–632 C.E.) in his lifetime. Twelver Shias hold that the twelfth imam is in hiding but will return to the world bringing peace and justice.

tyranny Rule by a tyrant, a man who used his wealth to gain a political following that could take over the existing government. In ancient Greece, tyranny was an illegal seizure of government but not necessarily a negative one.

U

ulama Scholars learned in Islamic scripture and law codes whom Sunnis trust to interpret the Quran and the Sunna. *See also* Sunni.

umma The worldwide community of believers in Islam. Muhammad's (ca. 570–632) emphasis on loyalty to the whole of the umma over the individualism of the tribe allowed Islam to serve as a binding force for the converted.

UN *See* United Nations.

unequal treaties A series of nineteenth-century treaties in which China made major concessions to Western powers, losing control of Vietnam, Korea, and Taiwan and allowing other countries to establish military bases, extract raw materials, and build railroads within China.

unilateralism A foreign policy in which a nation takes action in its own interest regardless of disapproval from allies. The United States moved unilaterally when it decided to invade Iraq in 2002, despite dissent from other members of the United Nations.

United Nations (UN) An international peacekeeping organization and forum for international opinion, established in 1945 at the end of World War II (1939–1945). Beyond international peace, its mission includes developing friendly relations between countries, solving conflicts through negotiations, and promoting social and economic development.

Universal Declaration of Human Rights A declaration adopted in 1948 by the United Nations that affirmed the inherent dignity of all human beings and charged nations that signed to respect specific human rights as detailed in the document.

universal religion A religious tradition that claims to be open to everyone and that actively seeks converts. It usually refers to Buddhism, Christianity, and Islam.

university Medieval European centers of scholarship and learning restricted to men and providing valuable services to kings and popes. Universities originally developed in the thirteenth century as guilds of students and masters in places such as Paris,

Bologna, and Oxford. In the modern era universities became the site of critical scientific, technological, and sociological research, and some began admitting women in the late nineteenth and early twentieth centuries.

Untouchables *See* outcastes.

Upanishads Indian mystical and philosophical works, written between 800 and 400 B.C.E. by mostly anonymous thinkers. Although the new doctrines contained in the Upanishads were intellectually revolutionary, in social and political terms they reinforced the existing power structure in India.

urbanization The process by which formerly rural areas and small towns and cities grow in size and population. Beginning in the nineteenth century and fueled by industrialization, city populations in Western nations dramatically increased—nearly doubling in some countries—by mid-century, as people sought factory and other jobs in new urban centers. In much of Latin America, Africa, and Asia during the nineteenth and twentieth centuries, urbanization occurred without much industrialization.

usury The practice of charging interest on loans, forbidden under Christian and Muslim legal codes.

utilitarianism A liberal ideology promoted by English philosopher Jeremy Bentham (1748–1832), which argues that the best social and political policies are those that produce the greatest good for the greatest number and are therefore the most useful.

utopian socialism A plan developed by French and British thinkers early in the nineteenth century that envisioned the creation of a perfect society through cooperation and social planning. Karl Marx (1818–1883) and Friedrich Engels (1820–1895) coined the term and argued that such a society was not sustainable because the interests of the working and middle classes were inevitably opposed to each other. *See also* Marxism.

V

Vaisya The major Indian caste grouping that was originally defined as farmers but eventually included merchants. *See also* caste system.

varna Another name for the four strata, or groups, into which Indian society was divided under the caste system. People belonged to one of four varna as a result of their birth. *See also* caste system.

vassalage A system of obligations, rights, and duties a free person (or institution) owed to the individual or entity upon which he (or it) was dependent. Rulers of the Zhou dynasty in China (1050–256 B.C.E.) employed relatives and trusted subordinates, or vassals, to supervise conquered territories. Vassalage developed in ninth-century Europe in response to a lack of central authority; as power increasingly fell into the hands of local lords, these lords required vassals to defend them.

Vedas Early collections of Indian hymns, songs, and prayers that contain sacred knowledge and were initially preserved in oral form. They were recorded in writing around 600 B.C.E.

Velvet Revolution The 1989 ousting of Czechoslovakian Communist bosses in only ten days. It grew out of popular demonstrations led by students, intellectuals, and a dissident playwright, Vaclav Havel (b. 1936), who was then elected as president.

Venus figurine A Paleolithic carving of the female form, often with exaggerated breasts, buttocks, hips, and stomach, which may have had religious significance. Some scholars believe the prevalence of Venus figurines indicates that the religious beliefs of Paleolithic peoples had a strongly feminine dimension.

vernacular language The language spoken by ordinary people as opposed to a written, scholarly language. Vernacular literature began to flourish in fourteenth-century Europe (replacing works published in Latin) and sixteenth-century China and included short stories, novels, plays, and poetry.

vertical archipelago The Andean system of planting and grazing at different altitudes. Terraces up the mountainside were shored up with earthen walls to retain moisture and enabled the growing of many types of potatoes.

viceroyalty The four administrative units of Spanish possessions in the Americas: New Spain, Peru, New Granada, and La Plata. Each was ruled by a viceroy in the name of the king and had its own court, or audiencia. *See also* audiencia.

vizier The caliph's chief assistant who advised him on matters of general policy, supervised the bureaucratic administration, and oversaw the army, the provincial governors, and relationships with foreign governments. The Abbasids, who acquired power over the Islamic territories in 750, borrowed the idea from the Persians. *See also* caliph.

W

waka (huaca) A sacred location, monument, or object in Andean cultures.

war communism The application of the total-war concept to a civil conflict. During the Russian Revolution (1918–1921), the Bolsheviks seized grain from peasants, introduced rationing, nationalized all banks and industry, and required everyone to work.

war guilt clause The part of the Treaty of Versailles (1919) that assigned blame for World War I (1914–1918) to Germany and forced the Germans to make monetary reparations. The clause was the source of much resentment in Germany, a fact the Nazi Party was able to use in bolstering its rise to power in the 1930s.

War Raw Materials Board An organization set up by the German government to ration and distribute raw materials during World War I (1914–1918) as part of the total-war effort. The board launched an aggressive recycling campaign, succeeded in the production of substitutes for rubber and nitrates, and strictly rationed food. *See also* total war.

Warring States Period The period of Chinese history between 403 and 221 B.C.E., when there was no central authority and political chaos reigned.

Warsaw Pact A cold war alliance formed in 1955 among the Soviet Union and its Eastern European satellite states (Bulgaria, Czechoslovakia, East Germany, Hungary, Poland, and Romania) as a counter to the North Atlantic Treaty Organization (NATO). It ceased to exist in 1991 after the collapse of communism in the Soviet Union and Eastern Europe.

water frame A machine, invented by Richard Arkwright around 1765, that used water power to spin coarse, strong thread and required large, specialized mills. The growth of these cotton mills marked the beginning of the Industrial Revolution in England.

Way of the Warrior See bushido.

Weimar Republic The weak government that replaced the German imperial state at the end of World War I (1914–1918). Its failure to take strong action against war reparations and the Great Depression provided an opportunity for the Nazi Party's rise to power.

welfare state A system comprising state-sponsored programs for citizens, including veterans' pensions, social security, health care, family allowances, and disability insurance. Most highly developed after World War II (1939–1945), the welfare state existed on both sides of the cold war; it intervened in society to bring economic equality by setting a minimum standard of well-being.

Westernization The effort to remake a country's government, economy, culture, and society in the image of Western European countries or the United States. Countries that attempt Westernization often meet with strong resistance from traditionalists, who want their native values to remain the same.

World Bank An international institution of credit created in 1945 with the intention of regulating the global economy, preventing another Great Depression, and stimulating economic growth, especially in the poorer nations. With the increasing globalization of finances and national economies and the dominance of capitalist nations, it has imposed free-market and pro-business conditions on poorer countries that want to qualify for loans.

World Trade Organization (WTO) An international body representing 149 nations that negotiates the rules for global commerce and is dedicated to the promotion of free trade. However, it has become a target of globalization critics who argue that the organization represents only the interests of global corporations. *See also* antiglobalization/alternate globalization.

World War I Also called the "Great War" (1914–1918); in essence a European civil war with global implications that was marked by unprecedented casualties, the expansion of offensive military technology beyond tactics and means of defense, and the massive mobilization of both troops and civilians on either side. This "total war" was ended by the Treaty of Versailles, the conditions of which only set the stage for World War II (1939–1945). *See also* total war, Treaty of Versailles.

World War II A war (1939–1945) with two major fronts: one in Asia, where China and the United States fought to contain

Japanese imperial expansion, and one in Europe, where a coalition of allies including Great Britain, the Soviet Union, and the United States fought to contain German imperial expansion. Significant advances in military technology and blurred lines between civilian and military targets resulted in 60 million deaths, more than half of them civilians.

WTO *See* World Trade Organization.

Y

Yalta Conference A pivotal meeting of Winston Churchill of Great Britain (r. 1940–1945, 1951–1955), Franklin D. Roosevelt of the United States (r. 1933–1945), and Joseph Stalin of the USSR (r. 1929–1953) in February 1945 that approved the establishment of the United Nations and granted the USSR considerable influence in Eastern Europe and elsewhere.

yangban Hereditary aristocrats at the top of the Korean social system who owned most of the land and held most government offices.

Yellow Turban Rebellion A major Chinese peasant revolt that began in 184 C.E. and helped cause the fall of the Han dynasty (206 B.C.E.–220 C.E.). Inspired by Daoist teachings, it sought to establish a new golden age of equality and harmony.

yin and yang An expression of the Chinese belief in the unity of opposites. One pole represents the feminine, dark, and receptive, and the other the masculine, bright, and assertive. The concept helped elite Chinese see Daoism as complementary rather than contradictory to Confucian values.

Yom Kippur War A conflict in October 1973 between Israel and several Arab states, led by Syria and Egypt. An attack on Yom Kippur, the holiest day in the Jewish calendar, took Israel by surprise; however, Israeli forces recovered and pushed the fighting into neighboring Arab nations. After two weeks of fighting, the United Nations arranged a cease-fire.

Young Turks Idealistic Turkish exiles in Europe and young army officers in Istanbul who seized power in the revolution of 1908 and helped pave the way for the birth of modern secular Turkey.

yurt A portable tent used as shelter by nomadic Mongols, who had no permanent houses. Before their great conquests beginning in the thirteenth century, Mongols moved with their animals in between winter and summer pastures, and yurts could be dismantled and loaded onto animals or carts in a short time.

Z

zaibatsu The huge family-controlled industrial enterprises that dominated the Japanese economy and worked closely with the government from the Meiji Restoration (1867–1868) to the period leading up to World War II (1939–1945). They were abolished in 1940 and were replaced by keiretsu after World War II. *See also* keiretsu.

Zamindar A landholding official who collected taxes from peasants in Mughal India for the emperor. When the British colonized India, the Zamindars became landlords to whom peasants paid rent.

zemstvos Regional councils of the Russian nobility established after the emancipation of the serfs in 1861 to deal with education and local welfare issues. While the zemstvos served as an attempt to modernize the government, they were ultimately suppressed by the tsar, who desired complete autocracy.

Zen Buddhism A form of Buddhism originating in China but developing most fully in Japan. It is noted for its emphasis on meditation. *See also* Chan Buddhism.

ziggurat A Mesopotamian stepped pyramid that marked the center of a city. Unlike an Egyptian pyramid, a ziggurat was a solid structure of baked brick, an artificial hill at the summit of which stood a temple.

Zionism A movement that began in the late nineteenth century among European Jews to found a Jewish state, spearheaded by Theodor Herzl, who started the World Zionist Congress in Basel in 1897. Adolf Hitler's attempted extermination of the Jews during World War II (1939–1945) prompted Western powers to support the idea and create the modern state of Israel in 1948.

Zoroastrianism A religion based on the teachings of the prophet Zarathustra (Zoroaster to the Greeks), which took hold in Persia and received a degree of state support during the Achaemenid dynasty (558–330 B.C.E.). Zarathustra proclaimed the deity Ahura Mazda to be the "father of Truth," the only god in existence, and the representative of good in an ongoing struggle against evil. Persian kings were Zoroastrians who believed themselves to be agents of Ahura Mazda on Earth.